Living Faithfully

Living Faithfully

*A Devotional Study
of the
Second Epistle of Peter*

by

J. ALLEN BLAIR

LOIZEAUX BROTHERS
Neptune, New Jersey

FIRST EDITION, JUNE 1961

THIRD PRINTING, FEBRUARY 1977

Library of Congress Catalog Card Number: 61-14600

ISBN 0-87213-047-9

PRINTED IN THE UNITED STATES OF AMERICA

Dedicated

to

the Members and Friends

of the

Calvary Presbyterian Church

of Charlotte, North Carolina,

to whom these messages were delivered

CONTENTS

INTRODUCTION

One cannot read far into the Second Epistle of Peter without sensing the theme of "Living Faithfully." Doubtless Peter had never forgotten his extreme failure to live faithfully at the time of his outspoken denial of Christ years before. As a warning to other believers, to help prevent them from falling into the same satanic trap, he writes this brief Epistle. He passionately admonishes all true Christians to beware of false teachers and apostasy and steadfastly to follow the Lord in a life of holiness and obedience.

The Epistle was written about a year after the first letter, approximately 68 or 69 AD. Probably, like the First Epistle of Peter, it was written to Jewish Christians scattered throughout Asia as the result of persecution. The circumstances are different now, however. Instead of enemies without the church, they seem to be within. False teachers were denying Christ—not only by unscriptural doctrines, but by inconsistent and impure living.

Not only was the Epistle written for the Jewish Christians, but we notice from the apostle's opening sentence that it was written to all Christians in general. In Peter's first letter the believers are recognized according to their geographical locations. In the second Epistle they are described on the grounds of their spiritual experience, "to them that have obtained like precious faith."

Like the rest of God's Word, 2 Peter has not been outmoded by time. It is still as pertinent and needful for the believer as when it was written. With defection from the truth of God so obvious on every hand, and with so little practical holiness by those who bear the name of Christians, we need to study 2 Peter, absorb its teachings, and heed its message. For those who have obtained the "like precious faith," Second Peter will be a source of challenge, conviction, and consolation.

J. ALLEN BLAIR

1.

REDEMPTION

"Simon Peter, a servant and an apostle of Jesus Christ, to them that have obtained like precious faith with us through the righteousness of God and our Saviour Jesus Christ: Grace and peace be multiplied unto you through the knowledge of God, and of Jesus our Lord."—2 Peter 1:1-2

In the opening words of this stirring Epistle, God's marvelous plan of redemption is suggested. Peter writes as "a servant and an apostle of Jesus Christ." He is no longer the same inconsistent Peter who denied his relationship to Christ years before. The careless, impetuous, profane fisherman has been delivered from his pride and selfishness by the redeeming blood of Christ. In his first Epistle he heralds the great fact of redemption by blood as a truth that must never be forgotten. "Forasmuch as ye know that ye were not redeemed with corruptible things, as silver and gold . . . But with the precious blood of Christ, as of a lamb without blemish and without spot" (1 Peter 1:18, 19).

Indeed, there is no message needed more in the world

11

of confusion and turmoil in which we live than the message of redemption through the blood of Jesus Christ. In Romans 3:24 God declares, "Being justified freely by His grace through the redemption that is in Christ Jesus." There can be no redemption apart from Christ. He was our sin-bearer and substitute who died on the cross, making eternal redemption possible for all who believe on Him. Those who believe on Him are forever redeemed. Those who reject or neglect Him are lost and condemned to eternal perdition. Have you received the Lord Jesus into your heart? Are you certain of redemption from sin? You can be. For Christ "gave Himself for us, that He might redeem us from all iniquity, and purify unto Himself a peculiar people, zealous of good works" (Titus 2:14).

Even the name, "Simon Peter," proclaims the message of God's wonderful redemption. The double name recalls the twofold aspect of the apostle's life—before and after redemption. "Simon" was the name given to him at birth following his circumcision. "Peter" was the name given to him at his rebirth following his conversion. After Peter's clear-cut statement of faith declaring Christ to be "the Son of the living God," as recorded in Matthew 16:16, our Lord gave him a new name. No longer was he to be known as the unstable, undependable Simon. He was a new creature in Christ. Our Lord said, "Thou art Peter" (Matthew 16:18), suggesting the rocklike nature and character that later distinguished God's servant from his former self.

One time a phrenologist, while lecturing in a certain town, declared his ability to tell anyone's nature from the bumps on his head. A rough-faced, stern-looking man mounted the platform. After a thorough examination of the subject, the lecturer described him as hard, cold, and possessed of many disagreeable traits. The audience laughed derisively, for they knew their neighbor to be kind, genial, and benevolent. Several told the professor he had miserably failed to judge character by his science. But the man himself understood. Turning to the people he said, "Friends, you have heard an exact portrayal of my nature before the Lord Jesus took possession of me. But since He came into my life, all has been different."

The same was true of Peter. It is likewise true of all believers. Before conversion all of us are in God's sight degenerate, sinful, and vile. But after conversion, through the indwelling Spirit, we are enabled to live holy, justly, and righteously.

As Peter wrote this second Epistle, he was nearing the end of his life. He was aware of this for he wrote in Chapter 1, verse 14, "Knowing that shortly I must put off this my tabernacle." Approaching the end he reminisces. He recalls the "Simon" life, but how grateful he is that it was supplanted by the "Peter" life. But though his conversion was instantaneous, his transformation was gradual. Peter, like most of us who have believed on Christ, was extremely slow in coming to the place of absolute and complete surrender to the Lord. More and more, however, as he grows older in the faith, he conforms unto the perfect likeness of Christ. In fact, the importance of this truth so gripped his heart that it is the final admonition he leaves with us in this last letter we have from his pen: "But grow in grace, and in the knowledge of our Lord and Saviour Jesus

Christ. To Him be glory both now and for ever. Amen" (2 Peter 3:18).

May I pause to ask, "Is there an old and a new to your life?" Have you definitely invited the Lord Jesus into your heart as your Saviour from sin? There is nothing more important for any of us than making this decision to receive Christ. If you have believed on Him, the Bible declares you to be a "new creature"; and as a result, "old things are passed away; behold, all things are become new" (2 Corinthians 5:17). If you are a Christian, your life should reveal your profession of Christ. Others should detect your conversion experience by the way you live. Your new life should evidence your new birth.

In his opening sentence, Peter gives himself the title of "a servant and an apostle of Jesus Christ." My, what potency there is in the gospel. Who would have thought one as impetuous as Peter could become such a usable tool for righteousness? There is no doubt that the gospel "is the power of God unto salvation" (Romans 1:16). There is no limit to what God can do through those who surrender their lives to Christ.

It is well to recognize that Peter denotes himself a "servant" as well as an "apostle." His was a special position as an apostle, but before mentioning that, he tells of his general position as a servant. Not all of Christ's followers are called to be apostles; but without question, all are called to be servants. By the order of the two words, Peter would have us see that the way up is down. He who would be useful to God must be willing to bow low. James stated it clearly when he wrote, "Humble yourselves in the sight of the Lord, and He shall lift you up" (James 4:10).

A Bible teacher, while driving up a hill from Oceanside to Vista, California, to speak at a conference, noticed a sign at the entrance of the latter town, "Population, 1,7500." It was quite obvious that some prankster had added the extra zero. Thus in his own mind, the Bible teacher whittled the town down to its true size.

Shortly after, in the pastor's study at the Community Church, the deacons prayed before the morning service. The first man to pray was a young convert. In his prayer he said, "Lord, we thank thee for our guest speaker, and for his reputation; but let us remember that no matter how big men are, they still need Thee." Immediately the Bible teacher remembered the roadside sign and realized that this young deacon was rubbing out any zeros that he or anyone else might have added. If we are to be servants for Christ, we need to be whittled down to our proper size.

How regrettable that many who name Christ as Lord are quick to recognize their position *in Him*, but fail to realize their obligation *to Him*. Every Christian is called to be a servant. Jesus said, "If any man serve Me, let him follow Me; and where I am, there shall also My servant be: if any man serve Me, him will My Father honour" (John 12:26). Let us not claim the dignity without the responsibility. We are servants of Jesus Christ. There was a time when we were servants of sin; but the Lord has redeemed us. Now we are His, not to live for ourselves, but for Him.

A Christian organization asked each officer to turn in a written report at every business meeting. The reports were to end with the words, "This work was done for the Lord Jesus Christ." The members accomplished much because that little sentence helped them to realize that they were serving not merely their company but their Lord and their God. How needful that believers do all their work in such a way that they can write beneath each day's record, "This work was done for the Lord Jesus Christ."

Please notice that the saints to which Peter writes did not *attain* the "like precious faith. They *obtained* it "through the righteousness of God." This is the message of redemption, which is purely of God's grace. None of us could ever do anything to *attain* salvation, "For by grace are ye saved through faith; and that not of yourselves: it is the gift of God" (Ephesians 2:8). A gift cannot be purchased or earned; it can only be received. The same is true of the gift of eternal life through Jesus Christ. It can only be received by believing on Christ. Actually the word "obtained" as used here means "to receive by divine lot or bestowment." God will bestow the gift on all who come to Him through His Son. He desires that all come, for He says in 2 Peter 3:9 that He is "not willing that any should perish, but that all should come to repentance."

Were it necessary to *attain* the "like precious faith" we might likewise lose it, if we fall short of the requirements for attainment. But since our redemption does not depend on our efforts, neither does the keeping of it. Praise God, the same Lord who saves us, keeps us saved.

Some would have us believe that it is presumptuous to be certain of salvation. How far such a thought is from the truth. The worst presumption of all is to doubt what God says in His Word. Does He not tell us in 1 Samuel 2:9 that "He will keep the feet of His saints"? We may stumble and fall, but God does not. No, it is not our hold on Christ that sees us through. It is His hold on us. "I give unto them eternal life," Jesus said, "And they shall never perish, neither shall any man pluck them out of My hand" (John 10:28). Thus, it is Christ's responsibility to keep us saved; but it is our responsibility to trust Him to do it. Our eternal redemption is not built on feelings or guesses. It is established on the sure foundation of the Lord Jesus Himself.

The "faith" Peter speaks about in these verses is distinctly different from the false faith of the heretics, the feigned faith of the hypocrites, and the fruitless faith of the mere professors of salvation. Peter declares it to be "precious faith." Why is it precious? First, because it is through faith that we become children of God (Galatians 3:26). There is no other way to come to the Lord. Secondly, without faith it is impossible to please God (Hebrews 11:6). Next, it is through faith that we enjoy all the promises of God (2 Corinthians 5:7). And then it is by faith that we receive cleansing from daily defilement (Acts 15:9). In fact, what phase of Christian living is not dependent on faith? We can best sum it up in the words of Romans 1:17, "The just shall live by faith." No wonder Peter declares it to be "precious faith."

"Precious" is a characteristic word in Peter's Epistles. He tells us trials are precious (1 Peter 1:7), the blood is precious (1 Peter 1:19), Christ is precious (1 Peter 2:7), God's promises are precious (2 Peter 1:4). The "precious faith" is the key that unlocks the door to all of God's wonderful treasures. The "precious faith" can only be received, Peter tells us, "through the righteousness of . . . Jesus Christ" who is both "God and our Saviour."

Second Peter is addressed "to them that have obtained

like precious faith *with us*." Peter is an apostle, having lived and worked with Christ personally, but he claims no unusual position in the body of Christ. He places himself on the same level with all who have been redeemed. The Apostle Jude, likewise, emphasizes the same thought as he speaks of the "common salvation" (Jude 3). Man makes his distinctions, but God declares that we "are all *one* in Christ Jesus" (Galatians 3:28). Faith in Christ gives the same privileges to all. God plays no favorites. How wonderful is His matchless grace!

Peter prays in verse 2, chapter 1, that "Grace and peace be multiplied unto you through the knowledge of God, and of Jesus our Lord." Such an experience is more than naming Christ as Saviour. It is claiming Him as "our Lord," the Master of all. Only as we daily yield to His full and complete control can we possibly know His all-sufficient grace and abiding peace. Peter informs us that such knowledge comes through Him, the Lord Jesus. May I add that it comes *only* through Him, for He is both grace and peace (John 1:17; Ephesians 2:14). That is why we must stay close to Him, not sometimes, but at all times.

The word "multiplied" suggests constant growth unto the fullness of the blessing of Christ. We are not full-grown; we are growing. As we feed upon God's Word daily, we increase our knowledge of Christ. As we learn more and more about Him, we increase our measure of His grace and peace. There is no other way. It must be through Christ, "In whom are hid all the treasures of wisdom and knowledge" (Colossians 2:3). He is the source of all things. "For in Him dwelleth all the fullness of the Godhead bodily" (Colossians 2:9). We are "complete in Him, which is the head of all principality and power" (Colossians 2:10).

It is quite certain that, if we do not grow in grace, we shall groan in disgrace. But the child of God who meets the requirements for growth, as set forth in the Scriptures, need not fear backsliding.

When Billy Sunday was just a young Christian, an old minister said to him: "William, if you will do these three things every day of your life, they will never write 'backslider' after your name: spend fifteen minutes a day letting God talk to you through the Bible, fifteen minutes a day talking to God in prayer, and fifteen minutes talking to someone else about God." Billy Sunday determined to do that, and "backslider" was never written after his name.

If you are one of the Lord's redeemed ones, having believed on Christ, you can rejoice with us in the "like precious faith." But should you be uncertain, may I urge you to "Examine yourselves, whether ye be in the faith" (2 Corinthians 13:5). And what is the test? Just this: "What think ye of Christ?" (Matthew 22:42) How you answer this question will be the difference between life or death, joy or sorrow, happiness or misery. Is Christ the Lord of your life, the One who died for your sins and rose again, who will someday come again to claim His own? If so, you are rejoicing in the "like precious faith." If not, you need Christ. Receive Him into your heart now.

2.

RECOGNITION

"According as His divine power hath given unto us all things that pertain unto life and godliness, through the knowledge of Him that hath called us to glory and virtue: Whereby are given unto us exceeding great and precious promises: that by these ye might be partakers of the divine nature, having escaped the corruption that is in the world through lust."—2 Peter 1:3-4

In the Doxology we sing, "Praise God from whom all blessings flow." How meaningful are these words. They portray one of the pinnacle truths of the Bible: God is the source of all that is holy, just, and good. James says, "Every good gift and every perfect gift is from above, and cometh down from the Father of lights, with whom is no variableness, neither shadow of turning" (James 1:17).

So often we puff up at our slightest accomplishment. We are so proud of ourselves. Glorying in our labors for the Lord, we overlook the true source of our achievement. "I have planted," Paul tells us, "Apollos watered; but God gave the increase" (1 Corinthians 3:6). Who gave the increase? God! Why then do we boast? What do we have that we have not received from Him? What lasting advance have we made apart from His power? "Our help is in the name of the Lord, who made heaven and earth" (Psalm 124:8).

Peter had been arrogant and pompous in his early days of fleshly service. Hear him when warned by our Lord of the betrayal: with self-righteous assurance Peter answered, "Though all men shall be offended because of Thee, yet will I never be offended" (Matthew 26:33). Poor Peter; like most of us, he forgot the frail insufficiency of the feeble flesh. He failed to realize that without the Lord's power and help the best of us are as weaklings before the enemy. How slow we are to comprehend the important truth of 2 Corinthians 3:5: "Our sufficiency is of God." We strive and scheme, but the Lord Jesus declares, "Without Me ye can do nothing" (John 15:5).

As Peter writes his second Epistle, he is cognizant of the many lessons learned over the years as a follower of Christ. But there is one very special lesson to which he gives due recognition in the verses for our present study. It was this essential truth that brought overflowing blessing to his heart, resulting in abundant usefulness for the Lord.

Peter is an elderly man now. No longer is he the self-centered, crafty individual he once was, motivated by the wisdom of the flesh. As we see him in his later years, he is God-controlled and God-directed, giving due recognition to the fact that God is the source of all blessing. Peter is convinced that there is nothing—absolutely nothing—inherently good in the flesh. Looking away from self, he would have every reader of his second Epistle understand that the Lord is everything—the only source of blessing. Like Peter, we would all do well to give proper recognition to this unalterable truth.

Peter writes, "According as His divine power hath given unto us all things that pertain unto life and godliness." Here the great fact is stated. Where do we get all things? The Scripture is clear—from the Lord Jesus Christ. His "divine power" is sufficient. The apostle further describes "all things" by stating that they "pertain unto life and godliness." Such a provision has no limits. What more do we need than "life and godliness"? The "life" spoken of here is spiritual life resulting from the new birth. If one has spiritual life, his most demanding need has been met. He can get along without riches, success, health, and many other things, but he will never know what real living is until he is born again by the Holy Spirit. In his first Epistle Peter declared, "Being born again, not of corruptible seed, but of incorruptible, by the word of God, which liveth and abideth for ever" (1 Peter 1:23). The moment one believes on Christ, he is born again and becomes the possessor of life, eternal life.

A young engineer accidently fell into a ten-foot water hole, deep in the Grand Canyon. He was marvelously rescued by a helicopter. Had it not been for the outside help he could not have been saved. There was a wall of rock on one side and a fifty-foot drop-off ledge on the other. For two long nights this young fellow anxiously awaited help. After being lifted to safety by his rescuers his comment was, "I feel as if I've been born again."

Needless to say he was grateful for the opportunity to

continue to live. He considered this to be a new birth. But the new birth spoken of in the Bible provides for far more than a few additional years on earth. The spiritual new birth results in eternal life, which knows no end.

The life received through the new birth is produced by Christ's "divine power," Peter tells us. As the young engineer had to be lifted from his trap by someone other than himself, so one can become a child of God only by divine intervention, the mighty power of God. The new birth results in a miraculous transformation the moment one believes on Christ. From this instant he is a child of the living God. John made this clear in his Gospel (1:12-13): "As many as received Him, to them gave He power [authority] to become the sons of God, even to them that believe on His name. Which were born, not of blood, nor of the will of the flesh, nor of the will of man, but of God."

The "divine power" not only produces new life in the believer, but "godliness" as well. Peter is very careful of the order of the two. He does not put "godliness" before "life," but rather "life," then "godliness." Some feel that by living like Christians they will become Christians. Thus, they work hard, trying to earn their salvation, seeking to gain the right to Heaven. "Not by works of righteousness which we have done," God tells us, "but according to His mercy He saved us, by the washing of regeneration, and renewing of the Holy Ghost" (Titus 3:5). "The washing of regeneration" refers to the cleansing away of all sin at the time of the new birth, while the "renewing of the Holy Ghost" has to do with the impartation of the divine life whereby we are enabled to live godly lives in Christ Jesus. It is impossible to live a life of holiness and obedience until we have received life from the Giver of life.

"Godliness" is the gift of God. As simply as one receives "life" through the "divine power" of Christ as a gift, so "godliness" must be received. In other words, our Lord does not expect the believer to *try* to live the Christian life. God desires that Christ be permitted to live through those who believe. Equally as impossible as saving ourselves is the task of living the Christian life. In the same manner in which the Lord gives eternal life at the new birth, He also desires to produce "godliness" or God-likeness in us. This is the life of victory whereby the believer permits the Lord Jesus to have the right-of-way to live not only in him, but through him.

In 2 Corinthians 2:14 Paul writes, "Thanks be unto God, which always causeth us to triumph in Christ." Literally this verse could read, "Thanks be unto God who always leadeth us in triumph in Christ." Praise God, there need not be defeat. Temptation and sin can be overcome. Christ gives victory to those who follow in the paths of His righteousness. As surely as the Lord saves the believer from sin, He will keep him from sin. David was certain of this fact, even though he had to learn the hard way after failing to trust the Lord fully. In Psalm 56:13 he says, "For Thou hast delivered my soul from death: wilt not Thou deliver my feet from falling, that I may walk before God in the light of the living?"

How wonderful it is that God does not merely save us and then let us struggle on the best way we can. "His divine power hath given unto us all things that pertain unto life and godliness." We have " all things" in Christ. We need nothing more. His strength, His power are ours as we believe Him and trust Him. Regrettably, however, too few of God's people appropriate Christ's divine power to live victoriously.

The story is told of a Welsh woman living in a remote valley in Wales who went to much difficulty to have electricity installed in her home. Since she was the only consumer in the entire area, the installation was extremely costly. When it was found that in three months her consumption was less than a unit, she was asked whether it was worth while.

"Indeed, yes," she replied. "I switch it on every night to see how to light my lamps. I then switch it off."

With almost unlimited light and power at her disposal, she still continued the weary grind of lamp trimming and filling, failing to use the time-saving and helpful electrical power to greater advantage.

Are not many Christians like this? Having been the recipients of "all things" through Christ's "divine power," they continue their toilsome and unavailing efforts to walk the Christian pathway in their own strength. Small wonder that they know so little of victorious Christian living. The power Christ has provided should be received and utilized. Horatius Bonar put it this way: "Believers are not hired servants, supporting themselves by their own work, but children maintained at their Father's expense."

Peter further informs us that though the Lord has "given unto us all things" essential for "life and godliness," we can best realize these possessions by taking time to be with the Lord. He uses the expression, "through the knowledge of Him that hath called us to glory and virtue." This is the second use of the word "knowledge" thus far. It does not suggest intellectual but rather spiritual knowledge of Christ. One may study the Gospels thoroughly and come away with a masterful grasp of the facts about Christ. But this is not the knowledge Peter has in mind. It is the knowledge that begins when Christ is received into the heart; knowledge that is developed and deepened as we daily commune with Him and rely upon Him for all things. As we increase our knowledge of Him daily, the "glory" and "virtue" to which we are called will become more and more obvious in holy living.

The apostle also tells us of something else included in the "all things" God gives His dear children, "whereby are given unto us exceeding great and precious promises." Specifically he has in mind the "precious promises" that have to do with salvation, such as the great passages in the Word calling sinners to repentance and faith in Christ. It is through these "precious promises" that we come to know of the Lord Jesus who provided eternal redemption for us. By receiving Him, we become "partakers of the divine nature." This is more than moralism or good works. We actually receive a new nature of righteousness, the nature of God. At the same time we are delivered forever from the power of sin, "having escaped the corruption that is in the world through lust." Paul writes in Romans 6:14, "Sin shall not have dominion over you." He does not say we are no longer sinners. The old nature is still with us, but through the strength of the living Christ we can live victoriously. Those born into the family of God by faith in Christ are enabled by the power of the Lord to overcome sin. "For whatsoever is born of God overcometh the world: and this is the victory that overcometh the world, even our faith. Who is he that overcometh the world, but he that believeth that Jesus is the Son of God?" (1 John 5:4-5)

Two travelers once asked an aged colored man a few questions in order to amuse themselves. They had just come to a fork in the road, and there was a signpost that read, "Liberty 40 miles."

"Sambo, how old are you?" they asked the elderly Negro.

"I guess I'se about eighty."

"Can you read?"

"No, sah."

"Can you tell us what is on that signpost?"

"Yas, sah; it says forty miles to Liberty."

"Well, now," said the travelers, "why don't you follow that road and get your liberty? It says there are only forty miles to liberty. Why don't you take the road and go there?"

The old man's countenance changed and he said, "That's a sham, young massa, but if it pointed up thar"— and he raised his trembling hand toward Heaven—"to the liberty we have when Christ makes us free, it wouldn't be a sham."

The old colored man, though uneducated, had experienced a liberty in his own soul of which many well-trained and well-taught Christians know very little.

Have you believed "that Jesus is the Son of God"? If so, there is no habit or sin you cannot conquer. We are "partakers of the divine nature." Certainly the divine nature is not sinful; it is sinless. We have "escaped the corruption that is in the world through lust." Literally this is "the corruption that is in the world as the result of lust." The unbridled "lust" of Adam and Eve brought condemnation to the entire race. Thus, without Christ, "There is none righteous, no, not one: there is none that understandeth, there is none that seeketh after God" (Romans 3:10-11). They are still lost in the bondage of their sins bound by "the corruption that is in the world."

God has not created us to die. He desires that we live, and not merely live, but live happily and joyfully. This is why "His divine power has given us all things that pertain unto life and godliness." In Christ we are possessors of His "divine nature." "We are more than conquerors through Him that loved us" (Romans 8:37).

Child of God, have you claimed your treasures in Christ? Have you placed the load of your sin completely on Christ? Are you enjoying the "liberty wherewith Christ hath made us free"? (Galatians 5:1) What is that sin in your life robbing you of peace and blessing? Bow before the Lord and claim victory. Recognize Christ's all-sufficiency; then fully trust Him.

And you who have never yet come to the Lord Jesus for salvation, may I beseech you to turn to Him before it is too late? Your greatest need in life is to be born again, to be born from above. Will you come to Christ now and receive Him as your Lord?

3.

RECIPROCATION

"And beside this, giving all diligence, add to your faith virtue; and to virtue knowledge; And to knowledge temperance; and to temperance patience; and to patience godliness; And to godliness brotherly kindness; and to brotherly kindness charity. For if these things be in you, and abound, they make you that ye shall neither be barren nor unfruitful in the knowledge of our Lord Jesus Christ. But he that lacketh these things is blind, and cannot see afar off, and hath forgotten that he was purged from his old sins."—2 Peter 1:5-9

In our previous study we recognized the fact that God "hath given unto us all things" in Jesus Christ His Son "that pertain unto life and godliness." In addition to this, believers are actually "partakers of the divine nature." But such provision does not exclude human responsibility. Those of us who have believed on Christ are not only to receive God's wonderful gifts. We are to use and develop them. Peter makes it quite clear, in the verses we are about to examine, that because of what God has done for us, we should be willing to *reciprocate* by expanding our spiritual gifts and graces. The Lord gives the fire, but we must do the fanning. At the same time by slothfulness and unconcern we may easily extinguish the flame.

"And beside this," Peter writes, "giving all diligence." That is, in view of the fact of what God has done for us, let us strive to do our part to co-operate in every way possible with His provision. This is the human side of the transaction. The words "giving all diligence" could also be translated "with intense effort." This suggests the seriousness and importance of our responsibility. We cannot expect to grow and abound in the "precious faith" without zealous endeavor. The Christian life does not merely happen. The Lord gives "all things" essential to "life and godliness." But after they are received, God's gifts must be used to glorify and magnify Christ.

Suppose someone gives you a gift of exquisite beauty and extraordinary value, wrapped and packaged most attractively. After thanking the giver you put the package away and leave it. In spite of its value, can you possibly enjoy the gift until you use it? So it is with God's gifts. If they are not used, they are of little value to us. By faithfully utilizing what God has given, we are assured of even greater blessing.

Considering the seven graces Peter mentions in verses 5-9, it is interesting to note that each one grows out of the previous one and, in turn, prepares the way for the next. The growth is not spontaneous. Toil and effort is demanded on our part or we shall be fruitless.

"Add to your faith virtue." This is the "precious faith" of verse 1. It is "the faith which was once delivered unto the saints" of which Jude speaks (Jude 3). We became possessors of this faith the moment we believed on Christ. Peter is not suggesting that we "add" to this faith in the sense of expanding or enlarging it. The "precious faith" is complete in itself. To "add" to it is to build upon it as one might add the superstructure of a house to the foundation. Jude expresses this idea when he says, "But ye, beloved, building up yourselves on your most holy faith" (Jude 20).

The first grace believers are called upon to add to their faith is "virtue." This refers to virtue in the moral sense. True faith in Christ always results in something. First in order, Peter tells us, is "virtue" or moral character. Consequently, those who know the Lord should prove their relationship to Him by holiness of life. "Faith, if it hath not works, is dead, being alone" (James 2:17). Dwelling in a world so devoid of moral character places the obligation on God's people more than ever to add virtue to faith. We have been called "out of darkness into His marvellous light" (1 Peter 2:9). Thus, in response to the divine gift of faith, God calls upon us to glorify Him with characters that are beyond reproach.

A little girl was spending a few days with her grandmother. While sitting on grandma's lap she said, "Grandma, I love you so much. You're so pretty!" The aged grandma, thin and wrinkled, laughed and replied, "That's very sweet of you, darling, but I'm not pretty." The little girl paused thoughtfully, then said, "Oh yes, you are. You are pretty on the inside."

God wants you and me to be "pretty on the inside." He wants us to be virtuous men and women, manifesting the holiness of Christ. His Word is clear: "Follow peace with all men, and holiness, without which no man shall see the Lord" (Hebrews 12:14).

"Virtue" is to be supplemented with "knowledge"; that is, knowledge obtained from the Word of God. Through believing on Christ we receive the "precious faith" which becomes the foundation for character. But from God's Word we get the wisdom that provides the instruction for character. "The Lord giveth wisdom: out of His mouth cometh knowledge and understanding" (Proverbs 2:6). We are not left to use our judgment as to right or wrong. God has provided clear-cut teaching in the Scriptures. To every student of the Word He says, "I will instruct thee and teach thee in the way which thou shalt go: I will guide thee with Mine eye" (Psalm 32:8). The more time we spend with God's blessed Word, the greater will be the desire for holiness and character. Not only does the Word challenge and inspire us, it cleanses and purifies. "Now ye are clean," Jesus said, "through the word which I have spoken unto you" (John 15:3).

Elwyn Davies, in the interesting missionary journal *Progress*, issued by the Bible Christian Union, says that while in Czechoslovakia recently he "sought in vain for a bookstore where it would be possible to purchase a Bible or New Testament." He further states that he "was told by believers there that they had not seen a new copy of the Word of God in the last ten years, that none are permitted to be printed in the country, and that the authorities will not allow any to enter the country. Many believers have no copy of the Bible these days, and as old copies wear out, the percentage of Bibleless Christians increases. The bookstores are full of technical books dealing with engineering, industry, agriculture, and, of course, matters pertaining to communist party activities."

It is a tragedy not to have a copy of God's Word to read, but it is a greater tragedy to have not only one copy, but several different translations of the Scriptures, and to neglect to read them. How greatly the condemnation rests upon Christians in the free countries who have the Bible in their possession but fail to make regular and consistent use of it. Remember, God says, "The entrance of Thy words giveth light; it giveth understanding unto the simple" (Psalm 119:130). Let us take time to add "knowledge" to "virtue" by poring over God's precious Word, permitting Him to speak to our needy hearts.

"Temperance" is the next grace Peter names. The word means "self-control," referring to the mastery of desires relative to sensual passions. It has particular reference to the control of the sex passions. How many Christian leaders have fallen to Satan's delusive schemes because of their failure to curb the appetites of the flesh. Recently, in one day, I heard of three outstanding Christian workers, in different phases of the Lord's work, ruined because of their failure to recognize this essential grace of temperance—self-control. The unsaved do not have the power to curb their sensual appetites, but Christians do. Peter mentions the "divine power" in verse 3. Indeed this power is for believers but it must be utilized. To all who have come to Christ, God says, "Let not sin therefore reign in your mortal body, that ye should obey it in the lusts thereof. Neither yield ye your members as instruments of unrighteousness unto sin: but yield yourselves unto God, as those that are alive from the dead, and your members as instruments of righteousness unto God" (Romans 6:12-13). These verses give us the secret of victory: yield not to sin, but yield to God. Complete surrender to the Lord Jesus is basic for victory over lust. The yielded life is assured of continuous victory.

Next to "temperance" Peter mentions "patience." Temperance has to do with the temptations that spring up from the inside of the believer while patience faces those from the outside. The word Peter used for "patience" could also be translated "endurance." Paul tells us to "endure hardness, as a good soldier of Jesus Christ" (2 Timothy 2:3). We are to persevere patiently, regardless of what temptations or testings God may permit to come our way. Most of us will agree that it is impossible to become a full-grown man in Christ without patience. Of course, the price for patience is costly. It does not come easily. "Tribulation worketh patience," Paul tells us in Romans 5:3. Let us not expect an easy road; life is a struggle from the cradle to the grave. We are engaged in a constant battle against the world, the flesh, and the devil. How necessary that we patiently endure all things, wholly relying on our wonderful Christ.

To "patience" we are to add "godliness"—reverence. I have heard God referred to on occasion as "the old man upstairs." Thoughtless jokes about Scripture are frequently heard in Christian circles. Empty choruses with far more jingle than message are sung in many places. Frequently, praying sounds as though the man on the street is being addressed rather than God. But even the seraphim who live in the presence of God cover their faces and cease not to cry, "Holy, holy, holy" (Isaiah 6:3).

An actress who sings and dances in a Broadway night-club recently told a reporter, "When I go on stage, I speak to God and say, 'You are on now; it's up to you.'" What blasphemy! What a perverted conception of God she has. But what about us? Have we added "reverence" to our faith? Do we respect and honor the Lord and give Him His rightful position of authority and power in all that we say or do?

We need to think, too, of the importance of reverence in the house of God. The moment some worshipers enter the sanctuary, they bow their heads and commune with the Lord. Throughout the service they think only of Him and His message for them. Others come to visit with their friends and talk. Their thoughts are concentrated on what they see about them and what they plan to do throughout the rest of the day. They leave the service with very little but criticism. They receive little because they invest little.

A Christian young man was visiting in a church in the west. Just behind him sat two women who whispered continuously throughout all the early part of the service. Soon babies and small children were brought to the front of the church to be dedicated. One child, little more than a toddler, was restless and noisy. Promptly, one of the ladies in the pew whispered to her companion, "That boy should be spanked." In perfectly controlled tones, the visiting youth turned to them and said, "I think people who talk in church should be spanked." Not another whisper was heard from them during the remainder of the service.

How needful is this grace of reverence in the house of God. Oh, for a new atmosphere of meditation and worship in our churches. We need desperately to study to be quiet. Let us not forget to add "reverence" to our "patience."

To "reverence" God would have us add "brotherly kindness." Christians are to be kind to everyone but especially to other Christians. Paul stresses this in Galatians 6:10 saying, "As we have therefore opportunity, let us do good unto all men, especially unto them who are of the household of faith." The true Christian will show his kindness not only by words, but with deeds that back up the words. He will not wait until asked to help, but with a heart overflowing with love he will seek occasions to reveal kindness. He will show forth kindness not only to those who are kind to him, but to those that are unkind as well. In his first Epistle Peter writes, "Love as brethren, be pitiful, be courteous: not rendering evil for evil, or railing for railing: but contrariwise blessing" (1 Peter 3:8-9).

Coming to the end of his list of seven graces Peter reminds us that "charity" must be added. This has a broader connotation than "brotherly kindness." "Charity" is universal love. It is the divine love implanted in the heart of the believer by the Holy Spirit at conversion. Both "brotherly love" and "charity" are distinguished in 1 Thessalonians 3:12, "The Lord make you to increase and abound in love one toward another, and toward all men." Christians are to love each other and help each other, but they are to love the unsaved, also. They are to love the unsaved as God loves them, with a holy concern to see them won to Jesus Christ.

Thus we see seven important graces that are to be added to the "precious faith" received through Christ. Seven is the perfect number. When added to faith, these graces lead onward to the perfect image of Christ. They have their roots in faith and culminate in love. All seven of the graces, being the result of faith, should eventuate in love; more love for Christ and more love for others.

These seven graces are likewise seven steppingstones to enable us to know Christ better. "For if these things be in you, and abound, they make you that ye shall neither be barren nor unfruitful in the knowledge of our Lord Jesus Christ."

God's gifts always result in fruit. When cared for properly and consistently, they produce more fruit. No fruit is as important as knowing Christ better. This was Paul's constant desire, "That I may know Him" (Philippians 3:10). This should be our supreme desire. And how do we come to know Him better? By permitting these important graces to "abound" by diligent obedience to His will. Jesus said, "If any man will do His will, he shall know" (John 7:17). There are no short-cuts. Knowledge of Him comes by obeying Him.

Suppose these graces do not appear in the believer's life. The Scripture is clear, "He that lacketh these things is blind, and cannot see afar off." He lacks spiritual perception and vision, even forgetting the mighty work of grace in his heart when God delivered him from his sins. What is the message for us? If we do not go forward, we go backward. If we do not continually seek more spiritual truth we shall probably not desire any. Either we advance or retrogress.

God has been good to us. He has given us the faith out

of which these graces grow. Let us be diligent. Let us reciprocate by "giving all diligence" to add these essential graces to our faith.

If you have never received Christ into your heart, will you do so now? You cannot live the Christian life until you become a Christian. You can only become a Christian be inviting the Lord Jesus into your heart. Will you ask Him to come in?

REALIZATION

"Wherefore the rather, brethren, give diligence to make your calling and election sure: for if ye do these things, ye shall never fall: For so an entrance shall be ministered unto you abundantly into the everlasting kingdom of our Lord and Saviour Jesus Christ."—2 Peter 1:10-11

Peter calls every true, blood-bought child of God to the realization of a paramount truth. Simply stated, it is this: if you are saved, *prove it*. The great danger among Christians is *verbalism*—*saying*, but not *doing*. Verbosity is not enough. The "precious faith"—if it is genuine—must find its way out of the believing heart into convincing actions. Saying we are Christians may satisfy some; but if we are to assure emptyhearted and restless souls all around us that the gospel of Christ is the power of God unto salvation, we must present the evidence of holy and consecrated living. The apostle leaves no doubt about this as he says, "Wherefore the rather, brethren, give diligence to make your calling and election sure."

"Wherefore" refers back to verses 5-9. It is as though

Peter is saying, "Because of what I have just said relative to the believer's human responsibility of adding to or building upon the 'precious faith,' substantiate your divine call and election to salvation by doing all these things."

The "calling and election" of which Peter speaks has to do with the divine side of salvation. The Scriptures clearly teach that "salvation is of the Lord" (Jonah 2:9). It is a divine work of grace in the heart of the believing sinner whereby God completely forgives him of all sin and at the same time provides a new nature of purity and righteousness. The invitation to this experience is to "whosoever will." There are no exceptions. God is no respecter of persons. He desires that all come. This is made plain in 1 Timothy 2:3-4, "For this is good and acceptable in the sight of God our Saviour; Who will have all men to be saved, and to come unto the knowledge of the truth." God longs for everyone to believe on His beloved Son for salvation—young as well as old. Age is no barrier. The smallest child, if he is old enough to love his mother and dad, is old enough to love Christ.

A little girl by the name of Rose Mary was an attendant at Bible School meetings conducted by the Canadian Sunday School Mission. She was only six years of age and there was doubt about the benefit she would receive from attending. On the closing day of the meetings, opportunity was given for any who wished to receive Christ to come to the front. Rose Mary left her seat, but one of the teachers said, "Perhaps you don't fully understand, Rose Mary; you are so young; you'd better go back to your seat." Rose Mary went back, her heart full of anguish that overflowed in tears. Questioned by the teacher as to the cause, the child who was thought too little to understand sobbed, "My parents don't want me to be a Christian and now teacher doesn't want me to be one either." Rose Mary and the teacher knelt together in the schoolroom, and in just a few minutes a little child was born into the kingdom of God.

Is this not a living example of the word of our Lord as recorded in Matthew 11:25, "I thank thee, O Father, Lord of heaven and earth, because thou hast hid these things from the wise and prudent, and hast revealed them unto babes." The gospel of Christ is for the "babes" as well as the gray heads, and all in between. The question is: Have you come to the Lord Jesus Christ for salvation? If you have not, I pray that at this very moment you will receive Him into your heart by faith.

If you have believed on the Lord, you are unquestionably one of God's very own, called and elected to salvation by grace. This being true, Peter tells us that we are obligated to make our "calling and election sure." By deeds of kindness, by hearts overflowing with love, by purity and holiness, we are to reveal Christ to all with whom we associate.

A minister relates a story about Jacob Walker, a lighthouse keeper on Robbin's Reef off the rocky shore of New England. After years of faithful service of minding the light he became ill and died. His wife buried his body on the hillside above the shore on the mainland, in plain view of the lighthouse. Later she applied for and received the appointment as the keeper of the lighthouse. For twenty years she carried on alone, and then a New York reporter went out to get her story. She told him this: "Every evening I stand in the door of the lighthouse and look across the water to the hillside where my husband's body is buried. . . . I always seem to hear his voice saying, as he often said when alive, 'Mind the light! Mind the light!' "

Across the troubled waters and the roaring breakers of the confusing age in which we live, there comes another voice to you and me. It is the voice of the Son of God saying, "Mind the light! Mind the light!" This is the gospel light. We mind it by how we live and by what we say. Our Lord declared in Matthew 5:16, "Let your light so shine before men, that they may see your good works, and glorify your Father which is in heaven."

Peter further assures us that, if we make our calling and election sure, we "shall never fall." This could also be translated, "We shall never stumble." That is, as we faithfully build upon the foundation of the "precious faith" by consistently adding the graces Peter mentions for growth in the Lord, we shall never stumble back into the old pathways of sin. God will keep us going forward for Him. But the condition for victorious advancement in the faith is clear: "If ye do these things." The divine work of grace under no circumstances renders human effort unnecessary. It is true that we can live for the Lord only as He gives us the enabling grace, but this grace will be given to none other than those who have receptive and willing hearts. God has done His part and He continues to do so. Thus, if we are to reap the blessing, we must do our part. We must diligently make our calling and election sure by doing the things that will keep us from faltering and stumbling along the way.

The Lord Jesus says in John 13:17, "If ye know these things, happy are ye if ye do them." In essence this is the same truth Peter is emphasizing in our text, "If ye do these things, ye shall never fall." We must never overlook the importance of "doing" in its relationship to "believing." For one to say he believes on Christ without producing any visible evidence of belief is to pour confusion on believers all around us. The unsaved are already blinded by Satan; and when Christians live inconsistently, the situation becomes even worse.

The early Christians had several favorite sayings that were commonly spoken among them. Usually when they met on the street, in the market place, or in the church, one would exclaim to the other, "The Lord is coming!" What a splendid and profitable way for Christians to begin their conversation. Most of us have had the experience of spending an entire evening in the presence of those who called themselves Christians. Nothing was said all evening that even suggested that they belonged to the Lord. In fact, we felt almost embarrassed to say anything about the Lord. This was unknown among the early followers of Christ. They loved Christ and because of this they were constrained to grasp every opportunity to speak about the things that honored Him.

Another faithful saying among the saints of old was that stated by Paul in his letter to Titus, "This is a faithful saying, and these things I will that thou affirm constantly, that they which have believed in God might be careful to maintain good works" (Titus 3:8). Paul exhorts Titus to make frequent mention of this important truth, affirm it constantly.

Is it not true that in our present day we still need constant reminding that we who are in Christ must "be careful to maintain good works"? It is easy to "talk" Christ, but the Word of God enjoins us to "live" Christ. If we expect to win those we meet in our daily contacts, who have not yet come to our Saviour, it is imperative that we reveal Him in our manner of life. There is no stronger argument for the power of the gospel than to see the miraculous effects of God's message reproduced in sincere, holy, and abundant Christian living. Those who really live for the Lord have discovered on occasion that even though there was no opportunity to speak for Christ, the consistent, faithful witness of their lives was the means of drawing others to the Saviour.

During the Great War, a shipload of Hindus was sent to France. A number of Christian workers had been assigned for welfare work among them, with strict orders that they would not at any time mention the name of Christ or Christianity. Because they could not speak for their Lord, the challenge came to these Christians to so live before the Hindus that their lives would prove to be a persuading testimony to the power of the gospel. They literally followed the example of our Lord in the most menial things, washing the feet of the men in need, and ministering to them in every way possible in a living, though wordless, message. After experiencing this treatment for a while, the Hindu soldiers wrote home to their loved ones: "When we left Calcutta there were no Mohammedans who cared for our souls; there were no Buddhists who looked after us. These Christians have been brothers to us. There is nothing they have not done for us. They have been like servants. Put our sons and daughters in the missionary schools; we want them to know what this Christian religion is."

Nothing can be more effective for the Lord than holy and sacrificial living. It is this thought that Paul presents in Romans 13:14 when he says, "Put ye on the Lord Jesus Christ, and make not provision for the flesh, to fulfil the lusts thereof." To put on the Lord Jesus Christ means literally "to be clothed with Him"; letting Him permeate our entire being to the extent that those around us will know without question that a mighty work of grace has transpired in our hearts.

After Peter reminds the believer of the importance of proving his profession and calling by the "good works" test, he assures us that obedient and righteous living will never be overlooked by God, "For so an entrance shall be ministered unto you abundantly into the everlasting kingdom of our Lord and Saviour Jesus Christ." In other words, if the child of God is loyal and faithful to Christ in consistently adding the graces of growth outlined by Peter in the opening verses of the Epistle, his entrance into the kingdom will be triumphant and victorious. This is not to say that one's admittance into Heaven depends on how he lives. God makes it clear in His Word that there is no question about going to Heaven for those who fully trust in the Lord Jesus Christ. It is rewards, not salvation, that the apostle has in mind at this point in his Epistle.

We need to distinguish between those who will barely enter Heaven and those who will enter abundantly. Paul makes this distinction in his first Epistle to the Corinthians: "If any man's work abide which he hath built thereupon, he shall receive a reward. If any man's work shall be burned, he shall suffer loss: but he himself shall be saved; yet so as by fire" (1 Corinthians 3:14-15). The one who receives "a reward" is the faithful saint who spends his time serving the Lord and living for Him. His will be an abundant entry into Heaven. But the one who is saved "yet so as by fire" is the believer who enters into the presence of his Lord empty-handed. Though saved, he has carelessly lived for himself, giving little thought to righteous living or the needs of the lost. He reaches Heaven, but that is all. Both of these Christians go to Heaven on the grounds of the sacrifice of Christ for their sins; but one will hear the voice of the Lord Jesus saying, "Well done, thou good and faithful servant" (Matthew 25:21), while the other will be faced with the regretful memory of wasted years and fruitless living.

The Bible has much to say about the rewards that God is reserving for His obedient and devoted followers. In 2 Corinthians 5:10 Paul tells us that "We must all appear before the judgment seat of Christ; that every one may receive the things done in his body, according to that he hath done, whether it be good or bad." This is the believer's judgment, not for sin but for works. At the judgment seat of Christ, great hosts of God's redeemed people who spent their entire lifetime living for self will be faced with shame and regret. But those who claimed the God-given victory on earth and supplanted the self-life with the fullness of Christ will be eternally rewarded.

There will be many crowned heads in Heaven. There will be crowns of life for those who loved the Lord on earth in the midst of trials and testings and were faithful unto death. There will be crowns of righteousness for those who loved His appearing and who were persecuted, yet fought a good fight and finished their course. There are, too, crowns of glory for those who worked under the Chief Shepherd in feeding His flock, people like Sunday school teachers and ministers. It is wonderful to think of the poor, the hard-worked, the overlooked, and the unappreciated believers here who will receive their due recognition in glory. The judgment of Christ will be righteous judgment; everyone will "receive the things done in his body, according to that he hath done."

This being the case, does it not behoove all of us to give immediate thought to the future? Time passes so quickly. The older we get, the more we realize this. Some of us have been Christians for ten, fifteen, or twenty years and some even longer. Have we really been living for the Lord? Has ours been a life of implicit sacrifice for Christ? Were we to enter into the presence of our Saviour in the next moment would He be able to say, "Well done, thou good and faithful servant"?

Praise God, it is not too late to do something about this. What should we do? Consider the words of our Lord as they are recorded in John 12:24: "Verily, verily, I say unto you, Except a corn of wheat fall into the ground and die, it abideth alone: but if it die, it bringeth forth much fruit." There you have it! Would you produce much fruit for God with the hope of an abundant entry into glory? Then die! Die to yourself; die to the flesh; die to all that turns your face from Christ. Bow at this very moment and commit your entire self to the Lord. Let Christ be more than a name on your lips; let Him be the Lord and Master of your life.

If you have not yet come to the Lord Jesus Christ for salvation, come before it is too late. If you have doubts as to whether or not you are saved, make sure of salvation now by believing on Christ. Take God at His Word as He says in Acts 16:31, "Believe on the Lord Jesus Christ, and thou shalt be saved."

5.

RECONSIDERATION

"Wherefore I will not be negligent to put you always in remembrance of these things, though ye know them, and be established in the present truth. Yea, I think it meet, as long as I am in this tabernacle, to stir you up by putting you in remembrance; Knowing that shortly I must put off this my tabernacle, even as our Lord Jesus Christ hath shewed me. Moreover I will endeavour that ye may be able after my decease to have these things always in remembrance."—2 Peter 1:12-15

Psychologists tell us that man never really forgets anything, that all he has learned is stored away somewhere in his mind. The problem, however, seems to be in the recalling process, in being able to reproduce any one of these millions of accumulated impressions at a given instant. Actually, Peter faced this problem realistically, many years ago. Three times in verses 12-15 of the first chapter of his Epistle, he uses the word "remembrance." He is convinced that there are some things that must never be lost in the storehouse of our minds, but must be kept foremost in our thinking. These things, which Peter has so ardently stressed in the opening verses of the Epistle, are essentials that must be considered and reconsidered many times if the child of God is to grow and abound in grace and power.

"Wherefore I will not be negligent to put you always in remembrance of these things," Peter says. He desires to be a faithful servant of the Lord. This involves more than imparting new truth; it demands constant reminding of the old. There is a tendency on the part of those who would teach and preach the Word of God to endeavor to keep presenting new truth. Likewise, those who listen clamor for something unusual or sensational. But the apostle informs us that the re-emphasis of old truth must not be neglected. An important part of the preacher's responsibility is not simply that of telling his flock new things, but also that of reminding them of the old. We forget so easily. Thus, we must give repeated consideration to the fundamental truths of the "precious faith" which we have received in Christ.

Peter goes on to tell us how important is the regular reconsideration of these fundamentals of the faith. He says, "I will not be negligent to put you always in remembrance of these things, though ye *know* them, and be *established* in the present truth." Even though we may know the truth and be grounded firmly in it, this is no indication that we cannot stumble and fall into error. Was this not the sad plight of some of the Galatian Christians? In his letter to them Paul wrote, "O foolish Galatians, who hath bewitched you, that ye should not obey the truth, before whose eyes Jesus Christ hath been evidently set forth, crucified among you?" (Galatians 3:1) Here were men and women who were wondrously transformed by the power of God, but they soon drifted into error. Why? Doubtless, they failed to emphasize and re-emphasize the fundamentals of the faith and the essential graces for growth that all believers need to hear repeatedly.

This is one reason why I believe it is so very important for God's people to be regular and punctual in their attendance at church. God says in Hebrews 10:25, "Not forsaking the assembling of ourselves together, as the manner of some is; but exhorting one another: and so much the more, as ye see the day approaching." Why are we entreated not to neglect faithful, habitual fellowship together to worship the Lord? Simply because in such gatherings the saints are put in remembrance of the basic truths that keep them strong in the Lord and in the power of His might. Satan knows this. That is why he thrusts every possible obstacle in our paths, in order that we might be tempted to neglect the needed fellowship with other believers in the house of God.

There are many excuses given for lack of church attendance. One man says, "I don't go to church on Sundays because I was never taught to go when I was young, so I didn't form the habit." Another man says, "I don't go to church on Sundays because I was forced to go when I was young and it grew distasteful to me." Is it not true that when one does not want to do a thing, one excuse is as good as another?

"Why were you not at church Sunday?" one was asked. "I had company," was the reply.

A school teacher was asked, "Why were you not at school Monday?" and she answered, "I had company."

A merchant was asked, "Why did you not open your store for business Monday?" and he answered, "I had company."

All of us know better than that. No teacher or merchant ever gave such an answer. Nobody ever gives that answer except those who miss church services. The reason is, whether they will acknowledge it or not, that they think the church service is of less importance than school or store. No teacher would think of such a thing as missing school because company came in just as he started to school; no merchant would fail to open his store because company stepped in; the reason is that the teacher and the merchant believe their work is important. Church attendance is important too. In fact, it is far more important than most of us realize. If we are to progress and move ahead in our Christian experience, we need the help of the teaching ministry of the church to put us in remembrance of the truths of God's holy Word.

Peter next informs us that until his dying day he proposed to give himself to the needed ministry of reiterating the fundamentals of the faith, "Yea, I think it meet [right], as long as I am in this tabernacle, to stir you up by putting you in remembrance." "To stir up" literally means to awaken or arouse, to render active, to stimulate. Actually what Peter desired was to get believers burning for God with a holy zeal and a concern for souls.

Is there not a noticeable need for zeal among most Christians today? Do we not need to be aroused and awakened from our slumber? We call ourselves Christians, but how few of us are motivated by an infectious zeal that cannot be withstood, even by the enemies of the cross. The church has become polite and reserved for fear of giving offense. But are we not losing ground? The enemy is closing in. While we "play church," the teeming millions crowd along the broad road that leads to destruction.

Our churches are suffering from a sorrowful lack of zeal and passion. Behind this lack has been a false psychology which minified the emotional nature and glorified the reason. This pagan psychology maintained that any display of emotion was a weakness, and not only so, but it was a deteriorating element in the personality, antagonistic to true intellectuality. It is this underlying pagan element which has produced a dry rot in our churches and, as a result, in our hearts as well.

One night a church building caught on fire. Practically all the people in the little town hastened out to see it. The pastor was shaking hands with various people along the sidelines. With surprise he said to one man, "Brother, this is the first time I have ever seen you at church." The man replied, "Preacher, this is the first time your church has ever been on fire."

When a church gets on fire for God, the people will usually come. A group of young ministers once asked John Wesley how to get big crowds like he had. Mr. Wesley told them, "Young men, get on fire for Jesus Christ and your congregation will come to see you burn." In Jeremiah 23:29 God asks, "Is not My word like as a fire?" And in Jeremiah 20:9 the prophet says, "His word was in mine heart as a burning fire." When the fire of God's Word begins to burn in our hearts, we may be sure we shall burn for the Lord.

Recall the Gethsemane experience of our Saviour.

There He was with the burden of our sins, which He assumed for us. He asked three disciples—Peter, James, and John—to watch with Him in the depths of His soul torment; yet we read, "He cometh unto the disciples, and findeth them asleep" (Matthew 26:40). A few feet away from them the Redeemer of the race was wrestling with the powers of darkness in agony too crushing to be measured by the human mind; nevertheless, they did not watch with their lonely Leader even for a few moments when their wakeful companionship would have meant much. But is this not our trouble still? How do we explain our lack of spiritual power? Sleepiness! On every hand we see the refusal on the part of Christians to face the challenges of faith. With softness, flabbiness, and drowsiness in place of zeal, strength, and vigilance, we are an easy mark for the enemy. Our churches need pastors and laymen who, with the Holy Spirit's fire burning within them, will get up early and stay up late, if necessary lose comfort, rest, and sleep to testify to the Son of God as man's only hope, spreading His message of blood-bought, cross-gained atonement, going out to the highways and byways, and in Jesus' name compelling sinners to come to their Saviour.

Don't be afraid of zeal. God says in Galatians 4:18, "It is good to be zealously affected always in a good thing." Never forget, we are not only in a fellowship, but also in a fight. As the enemy strikes harder and as the battle becomes hotter, the call seems to come louder: "Put on the whole armour of God, that ye may be able to stand against the wiles of the devil" (Ephesians 6:11). Get into the fight for God. The battle can be won. But be assured, no battle has ever been won without zeal. There is no time to lose.

Let us surrender ourselves completely to the task of living for the Lord at this very moment.

One day in 1951, a Christian editor boarded a Canadian Pacific Airlines plane at Vancouver enroute to Tokyo. He was greatly surprised to find that, apart from the crew, he was the only civilian on the plane. There were thirty-three American soldiers, armed to the teeth and due to be in Korea within a few hours. The need was so appalling and the demand so imperative that by any and every means soldiers had to be hastened to the front. These warriors were not officers, not highly skilled technicians, not men of wide experience. They were a very average lot of men. The man sitting next to the editor scarcely knew how to use his gun. But the United States government paid about $20,000 to get those thirty-three soldiers over to Korea to fill the gaps in our hard-hit divisions. The experience of these men was very limited. The expense of getting them over there was not considered. There was a war to be won and it had to be won at once or it would be lost in a few days.

I wish I had the words and the speech to convince sleeping Christendom today that there is a war to be won and it must be won at once or it will soon be lost. In many parts of the world, the gospel of Christ has been practically silenced. Those of us who still have our freedom must not use it for our own selfish exploits. We are God's! We have been purchased by the precious blood of Christ. In His power and strength we must go forth to serve, impassioned with the same zeal that impelled Christ to go to the cross for us. If we meet the conditions, victory is assured.

What Peter is saying to us is said with tremendous urgency. He writes as a dying man to dying men, "Knowing that shortly I must put off this my tabernacle, even as our Lord Jesus Christ hath shewed me." As an old man, he realizes that death is near. Twice he uses the word "tabernacle" in reference to his body. This could also be translated "tent." Peter realized, as did the Apostle Paul, that in this world we who love the Lord "have no certain dwellingplace" (1 Corinthians 4:11). Ours is a mere "tent" existence.

The sad tragedy of so many Christians is that they have forgotten that they are pilgrims on this earth, traveling through to their eternal home. They are more concerned about "mansions" here and now than about those Christ promised in the hereafter. As a consequence, they become so involved in the cares of this life that they are of little or no value in the Lord's service.

Someone tells of traveling along the coast of South America. While his ship lay at anchor, on one occasion, it became "lily-bound." In that particular climate, the growth of vegetation is very rapid. In a few days the vessel became the center of a great, floating island of beautiful lilies! They grew so fast that the chain holding the anchor became entangled. Soon the flowery mass caused the anchor to drag and the vessel began to drift in the wrong direction. Then the crew had a long and hard task. With cutlasses and hatchets they finally released their ship from the lilies.

How easy it is for Christians to become so entangled with the gay and golden flowers of riches and worldly pleasures that their lives drift in the wrong direction! We must keep ourselves free from the entanglements of this "present evil world." "For here have we no continuing city, but we seek one to come" (Hebrews 13:14).

Recently I received a letter from a dear saint of God who has been a faithful listener to our Glad Tidings broadcast from the inception of this radio ministry. This Christian friend has written to us many times. Her letters are always an encouragement and a blessing. She has been a shut-in for a number of years, but never complains. Her penmanship is beautiful, but I have noticed recently in each succeeding letter the handwriting seems more shaky. In the last letter I received, she wrote as follows: "At seventy-eight years, as the earthly dwelling grows frailer and weaker, and efforts to keep up necessary duties are so painful, it is a 'moment-by-moment' experience of His grace and strength that sustains me. Praise and rejoice in Him!"

This child of God does not have her eyes fixed on the world in which we live with all of its attractions, but on Christ and His righteousness. Should not this be the desire of every true believer? Like Peter of old, we should be ready at any time to leave our "tent" existence to go to our home in Heaven.

Though Peter faces death, and even tragic martyrdom, there is no trace of despondency in what he has to say. He simply reminds us of the incident that had transpired years before on the shores of Galilee when the Lord Jesus had prophesied the apostle's martyrdom. Our Saviour had declared of Peter, "When thou shalt be old, thou shalt stretch forth thy hands, and another shall gird thee, and carry thee wither thou wouldest not" (John 21:18).

Peter evidences no fear of the future. With dauntless

courage he presses on, doing the work of the Lord. He has in mind the spiritual welfare of those to whom he is writing. There are no traces of self-concern: "Moreover I will endeavour that ye may be able after my decease to have these things always in remembrance." He longs to make the most of every opportunity to herald the fundamentals of the faith. He is concerned that, even after he goes to be with Christ through death, the effects of his ministry will continue to challenge many to walk in the light as Christ is in the light.

Should this not remind all of us who have believed on the Lord Jesus to examine our own motives and ambitions in life? Why did God save us? Why are we here? Are we not His, to live for Him? Let us ask Him to warm our hearts with a holy zeal that will impassion us with a new and fresh desire to really count for Him.

Should it be that you have never trusted in Jesus Christ for salvation, may I urge you to turn to Him now? Trust Him as the Man in glory who died for your sins and rose again.

6.

RECOLLECTION

"For we have not followed cunningly devised fables, when we made known unto you the power and coming of our Lord Jesus Christ, but were eyewitnesses of His majesty. For He received from God the Father honour and glory, when there came such a voice to Him from the excellent glory, This is My beloved Son, in whom I am well pleased. And this voice which came from heaven we heard, when we were with Him in the holy mount."—2 Peter 1:16-18

Not only is it important to reconsider old truths but it is also worth while to recollect old experiences. It is good to stop occasionally and reflect on the past. Progress is made not only by looking ahead, but also by looking back. The experiences of the past can provide many steppingstones for the achievements of the future. Peter is mindful of this. He pauses to recollect several incidents that are worth while for all of us to think about as we retrospect with him.

May we remind ourselves again that the enemies of the cross attacked by Peter in his second Epistle were not the same as those of the first. Those mentioned in the first Epistle were outside the Church. They made no pretense

59

of being believers in Christ. In fact, they despised Christ and Christians. But in his second Epistle, the apostle is greatly disturbed because of the enemies within the church. They professed to be Christians, but their teachings and their lives denied their profession.

Just how the early Church degenerated into this sad state we are not sure. We can only speculate. Could it be that they fell into the same error that is so obvious in scores of our present-day churches? There is a prevailing tendency among many to feel that there is power in numbers. In other words, it is thought that the more members a church adds to the roll, the stronger it becomes. This may or may not be true. Usually it is not true. In the economy of God, power is not known through numbers only, but through surrender and submission to the Lord Jesus Christ. The church should be the force, not the field. It should be a body of consecrated believers banded together in the love of God for fellowship, prayer, and Bible study in preparation for the task of winning the lost to Christ, both at home and abroad. As far as usefulness for the Lord is concerned, it is far better to have a church of fifty members, completely yielded to Christ, than five thousand members, many of whom have never really opened their hearts to the Lord's control. The devil works through nominal Christians. This is how he gains a footing in churches. Evidently this was the cause of the severe problem in Peter's day.

One of the errors in doctrine which Peter sought to correct concerned the Second Coming of Christ. The truth of our Lord's return had been ridiculed and opposed by certain groups within the church. They had derided it as a myth. But Peter boldly declares, "For we have not followed cunningly devised fables, when we made known unto you the power and coming of our Lord Jesus Christ, but were eyewitnesses of His majesty." God's servant recollects his experience on the Mount of Transfiguration. There he saw Christ in all His majesty as every eye shall see Him when He shall come "in the glory of His Father with the holy angels" (Mark 8:38). Peter was an eyewitness of the Lord Jesus in all of His resplendent glory. No wonder he wrote so frequently about the Second Coming of the Lord Jesus. The false teachers were saying that the return of Christ was merely one of the several "cunningly devised fables" being propagated by some Christians. To them the "blessed hope" was nothing more than a cleverly written story without any factual basis. Peter knew better. He had a visual foretaste of what is yet to come.

It is interesting to note how many of the problems of the early Church are duplicated in the churches of our day. Of course, this is understandable when we realize that the same devil who deceived and deluded those in Peter's time is still working hard at the same old game now. His methods never change. And, since he is limited in his tricks, we might expect to find him using some of his same ancient, well-worn lies. The Bible says of him that "he is a liar, and the father of it" (John 8:44). Since his fall, there has never been a time when he was not a liar. He cannot be trusted. The biggest lie he seeks to disseminate is that God's Word is not dependable.

Thousands of years ago in the Garden of Eden when the devil tempted Eve, the argument he used was that God does not really mean what He says. Eve had declared that she had been forbidden to eat of the tree in the midst of the garden, lest she die. But the devil replied, "Ye shall not surely die" (Genesis 3:4). In other words, what he was saying was, "Go ahead and eat. You can't rely on God's Word." The devil is still spreading this lie. Many in our churches have believed it—especially concerning the great truth of the Second Coming of Jesus Christ. But God assures all of us that in spite of what we believe or teach in regard to the Second Coming, the Scripture is not only clear but true, "For yet a little while, and He that shall come will come, and will not tarry" (Hebrews 10:37). To those who would laugh and scoff at this fact of Scripture, God declares in Matthew 24:44, "Therefore be ye also ready: for in such an hour as ye think not the Son of man cometh."

There may be justification for differences of opinion concerning the details in connection with the return of the Lord Jesus to the earth, but there should be no differences among those who believe the Bible concerning the *fact* of His Coming. To deny the fact of Christ's Coming is to refuse to accept the Bible as God's infallible Word. Following our Lord's ascension, the angel of God declared, "This same Jesus, which is taken up from you into heaven, shall so come in like manner as ye have seen Him go into heaven" (Acts 1:11). Could anything be clearer than this? "This *same* Jesus"—the disciples were still gazing into the sky, watching this unusual event, the ascent of the resurrected Christ into Heaven. Suddenly they are informed by two angelic messengers that this would not be the end of our Lord's work on the earth: "This *same* Jesus . . . shall so come in *like manner* as ye have *seen* Him go into heaven." He went into Heaven bodily and visibly; He will return in the same manner.

Looking to the last book of the Bible, the book of the Revelation, we have God's concluding message to man. Ever since this divine record was given to John, centuries ago, Heaven has been silent. But let us not forget that last words are usually important words. Though the book of the Revelation is ignored by many, even Christians, it is a book that should be read frequently and studied intently. Those who give themselves to the prayerful reading of this sacred book of prophecy will reap the special reward God has promised in its opening chapter: "Blessed is he that readeth, and they that hear the words of this prophecy, and keep those things which are written therein: for the time is at hand" (Revelation 1:3). Don't neglect the study of this wonderful book. If you do, you will miss the intended blessing God is reserving for you.

But as we are thinking of the last book of the Bible, consider the concluding chapter; and not only that, but its closing message. Anyone who does any writing at all knows how important it is to use the last paragraph to summarize the basic theme, that the reader might be so impressed that he cannot possibly miss the point of the thesis. It seems that the Holy Spirit uses this same principle in the book of the Revelation. In verse 20 of the last chapter, just prior to the benediction, the Lord Jesus says, "He which testifieth these things saith, Surely I come quickly." The Apostle John, with a heart overflowing with joy, rejoins, "Amen. Even so, come, Lord Jesus." Christ's Coming could not be too soon for John. He longed for the return of his Lord.

In the final word we have from our Saviour, He makes it clear that He is coming back to earth. This is not merely a possibility but a reality. The word "surely" could also be translated "yes—it is true." In other words, God is assuring us that we may bank upon it, we may stake everything we have upon this unquestionable truth. Whether believed or not, the fact cannot be altered; the Lord Jesus is coming back as God says in Revelation 1:7: "Behold, He cometh with clouds; and every eye shall see Him, and they also which pierced Him: and all kindreds of the earth shall wail because of Him. Even so, Amen."

Not only was the return of Christ being denied by certain false teachers within the early Church. This was a serious indictment; but more than this, these same false teachers, though professing to be followers of Christ, were living in gross immorality. Doubtless one's attitude toward Christ's return will be reflected in his manner of life. There is no influence that is more effective in stabilizing the believer in a walk of holiness and obedience than the "blessed hope." God declares in 1 John 3:3, "Every man that hath this hope in him purifieth himself, even as He is pure." Those who are looking for their Lord to return will live accordingly. They will not busy themselves with the selfish pleasures and exploits of this life. Rather, they will be motivated in all that they do by the hope of Christ's glorious appearing.

One of the oft-quoted Scripture portions relating to the Second Coming of Christ is 1 Thessalonians 4:16-18: "For the Lord Himself shall descend from heaven with a shout, with the voice of the archangel, and with the trump of God: and the dead in Christ shall rise first: Then we which are alive and remain shall be caught up together with them in the clouds, to meet the Lord in the air: and so shall we ever be with the Lord. Wherefore comfort one another with these words." What comfort this marvelous passage has brought to God's people down through the years. It refers to the Rapture, at which time all true believers, both dead and living, will meet their wonderful Lord in the air, ever to be with Him.

Although Bible-believing Christians place such an emphasis on the thrilling truth which is so clearly presented in the last third of 1 Thessalonians 4, we almost completely overlook the first two-thirds of the chapter. What is the theme advanced in the first twelve verses? Holiness of life! Paul gives detailed admonitions concerning the purification of our hearts in anticipation of Christ's return. In other words, if we really believe that Christ is coming back, we shall live each remaining day until He returns in a manner that will please and honor Him. I am convinced that the low spiritual plane of so many in our churches is the result of the neglect of the teaching and the believing of the doctrine of the Second Coming of Christ. When God's people know about this stirring Scriptural truth and really believe it, sanctified living and spiritual power will follow.

There were two serious errors being taught in the early Church that are still common in many present-day churches. One of them made light of the Second Coming of Christ, while the other denounced His deity. Peter deals with both of these in the verses we are considering. His argument for the deity of Christ is not only clear and concise, but convincing and conclusive. "We were there! We saw! We know!" Could there be any stronger argument? This was not a dream, but a first-hand, actual experience. No one can argue a man out of his personal experience. We "were eyewitnesses of his majesty," Peter declares. Further, in speaking of the Lord Jesus Christ, he says, "For He received from God the Father honour and glory, when there came such a voice to Him from the excellent glory, This is My beloved Son, in whom I am well pleased. And this voice which came from heaven we heard, when we were with Him in the holy mount." Peter actually heard the voice of God declaring Christ to be the Son of God. No wonder the apostle was willing to die a martyr's death. One will not knowingly die for a lie; Peter was thoroughly convinced in his own heart and mind of the deity of Christ.

Perhaps someone will say, "Well, that is all right for Peter, but what proof do we have now that Jesus is the Son of God?" There are many proofs: His words, His sinless life, His miracles, His resurrection, and numerous others. But keep in mind also that God speaks to us today through His inspired Word just as authoritatively as He spoke on the Mount of Transfiguration. We may not hear His voice audibly as Peter did, but certainly He speaks to our hearts from the Scriptures.

In John 1:1 God says, "In the beginning was the Word, and the Word was with God, and the Word was God." Here Christ is called the "Word," or as we read it in the original, the *Logos*. This Greek word comes from a verb meaning "to speak." When a person speaks, giving the sum total of his thoughts concerning another person, he gives his concept of that person. God has spoken in the person of His Son. Thus, Christ is the Word in the sense that He is the total concept of deity. The definite article used before *Logos* denotes that Christ is unique in that He is the only true concept of God. Thus, He had every right to declare as He did in John 14:9, "He that hath seen Me hath seen the Father."

Further in the first chapter of John's Gospel we read that "the Word was made flesh, and dwelt among us, (and we beheld His glory, the glory as of the only begotten of the Father,) full of grace and truth" (John 1:14). The phrase "was made flesh" does not mean that Christ was made into a man, but rather, He became a man in addition to what He already was in His deity. Actually, He was deity clothed with humanity. This is only one instance of literally hundreds in the Scriptures where God the Father speaks of Jesus Christ as God the Son.

Why did Christ become man? He came to be our sin-bearer, that through Him we might have a way of salvation. But were there not many religions in the world? Were these not sufficient? They were totally inadequate. There needed to be a better way. God provided this way, as we read in Hebrews 1:2: He "hath in these last days spoken unto us by His Son, whom He hath appointed heir of all things, by whom also He made the world." God sent His beloved Son to earth to die on the cross and to be raised from the grave as the sacrifice for our sins and the firstfruits of our redemption. He did all this for sinful, undeserving humans like us, that we might be eternally saved. This is God's plan. There is no way to be saved other than through Christ the Son of God.

It is said that a learned scientist was an agnostic. He believed in a "Supreme Being" who created all things, but from his study of the handiwork of this Being he had come to the conclusion that God was so great and so far off that no man could hope to know Him. One day the scientist was walking in his garden and stopped to watch some ants at work in an anthill. He noticed that the ants seemed agitated as his shadow fell upon them.

"If only those ants knew how kindly I feel toward them," he thought, "they would not be disturbed at my presence." Pondering further on this idea, he found himself wondering if a man could ever communicate his thoughts to ants. Immediately he realized that this would be an impossibility. For a human to teach ants what man is like, and to convey his thoughts to them, he would have to become an ant! Then, like a flash of lightning, came this thought: "Why, that is exactly the situation which confronted the God of this universe. Infinitely high as He is above us in His being and in His power, to teach men to know Him and to know His thoughts it was necessary for Him to become a Man!" And there, in the quiet of his garden, that man of science, who had many times heard but rejected the gospel, bowed in the presence of the Lord Jesus Christ in humble submission, exclaiming in holy awe, like Thomas of old, "My Lord and my God!"

There have been various answers given to the question, "Why did Christ come into the world?" I am sure the best answer of all was that given by Himself in Luke 19:10: "For the Son of man is come to seek and to save that which was lost." Christ left the glories of Heaven to come to the shame of earth to pay the price for our sins, that all who believe on Him might become like Him. Irenaeus put it this way: "He became what we are that He might make us what He is."

Have you experienced His saving grace? Do you know Christ in your heart? Maybe you know about Him, but do you really know Him? Make certain that you are a child of God. Realize that you are a sinner and receive Him into your heart now. Then live for Him and serve Him, watching and waiting for His glorious return.

7.

REVELATION

"We have also a more sure word of prophecy; whereunto ye do well that ye take heed, as unto a light that shineth in a dark place, until the day dawn, and the day star arise in your hearts: Knowing this first, that no prophecy of the scripture is of any private interpretation. For the prophecy came not in old time by the will of man: but holy men of God spake as they were moved by the Holy Ghost."—2 Peter 1:19-21

Peter begins the first chapter of his second Epistle with the thought of "faith," but he concludes by giving attention to "fact." Some consider the two as opposites; but this is not the case in the Christian way of life. The "precious faith" of which Peter speaks in verse 1 is substantiated by the "sure word of prophecy" of verse 19. In other words, the faith which believers possess in Christ is not without fact. The Christian faith is well established upon the solid foundation of reality.

The apostle reminds us that "we have also a more sure word of prophecy." The prophecy of which he is speaking

70

is the Word of God for man, which is contained in the Book which we call the Bible. This is "a more sure word of prophecy" in the sense that it is firm and stable; it can be trusted and relied upon. In the Scriptures we have God's revelation of truth put into permanent form that all may know the eternal plan of the ages. The Lord continues to speak through the Bible, His infallible Word.

Suppose it were to be announced by the press, radio, and television that on a certain day at a particular hour God would speak from Heaven to all the peoples of the world. Do you think they would take the time to listen? Surely they would. Shops would be closed, transportation would be halted, schools would be dismissed in order that everyone might witness this rare occasion. Doubtless only a few would miss this exceptional opportunity to hear the voice and the message of God. But let us be reminded: God has spoken! In fact, He has nothing more to say to us at present. He has revealed His entire plan and purpose for mankind. Not only has He spoken, but He has seen to it that what He said was placed in a Book that every succeeding generation, until the return of Christ, might know the message of God.

The late Dr. Harry Ironside, who until shortly before his death was pastor of the Moody Memorial Church of Chicago, used to tell of one of his boyhood desires. As a lad, he was deeply concerned about his soul. While reading in the Bible about angels appearing to men, he went immediately to his room, closed the door and prayed, "O God, if You will only send an angel to reveal things to me I will become a Christian." Of course, no angel came. But as weeks passed, the young seeker came to realize that God had already spoken and that what He had said was recorded in His eternal Word. Later, young Ironside received the message of God into his heart, believed on Christ, and was saved.

Indeed, the Bible is "a more sure word of prophecy." It will continue to stand after everything else crumbles. In Isaiah 40:8 God declares, "The grass withereth, the flower fadeth: but the word of our God shall stand for ever." Because the Bible is what it is, Peter says, "Whereunto ye do well that ye take heed, as unto a light that shineth in a dark place." The Bible is more than an ornament; it is to be used.

Though the Bible has long been known as the "world's best seller," how widely is it actually read? Though it can be found in most homes in America, its contents seem to be little known. In a nation-wide Gallup poll, in which people were asked to name the first four books of the New Testament, only one person out of three could name all four; over half of the people were unable to name any of them. What a shocking revelation of the public's appalling ignorance of the Book of books! The four Gospels contain the story of our Saviour's birth, life, words, works, death, burial, resurrection, ascension, and promised return. If over half of our population is unable to name any of the first four books of the New Testament, how destitute these same people must be in their knowledge of the contents of these sacred books. Peter warns, "Ye do well that ye take heed." Read the Bible; believe the Bible; obey the Bible; this is the apostle's plea, "Take heed"!

God's Word is as "a light that shineth in a dark place." Probably at no time in history has the entire world been blanketed more by the darkness of confusion and distress than it is today. Who is not weighted down with burdens and problems far beyond the capacity of the human mind? We may be perplexed and bewildered; but, praise God, in the midst of it all there is a light: "Thy word is a lamp unto my feet, and a light unto my path" (Psalm 119:105). What would some of us have done, when we did not know which way to turn or what to do next, had it not been for the light we found in God's blessed Word? On the other hand, where might some of us have been today had we faithfully searched the Scriptures and obeyed them rather than followed the way of the flesh?

How important that those of us who know the Lord spend time poring over the pages of God's sacred truth. I wonder how many of us could say, as did God's servant in Job 23:12, "I have esteemed the words of His mouth more than my necessary food." Job considered the use of the Scriptures in his daily routine to be far more important than essential food for bodily sustenance. Evidently the Chinese Christian, Leland Wang, feels the same way. He has frequently said, "No Bible—no breakfast!" He is not willing to approach the breakfast table until he has first fed his soul upon the heavenly manna of the Word. Such a practice is commendable if we are to delight in God's best.

The Berean Christians "searched the scriptures daily" (Acts 17:11). I cannot help but feel that most of this "searching" was done in the early morning hours. Not only is this the best time because of the alertness of our minds, but it suggests to God our love and adoration for Him in seeking to keep Him in the place of pre-eminence the King of our hearts deserves. This is not to mention the scores of blessings we receive, such as comfort, guidance, inspiration, and many other essentials with which to face the uncertainties of the day. Do not rush off into the many activities of the day without taking time to prepare yourself adequately. Meditation on God's Word is a requisite for this preparation.

The "sure word of prophecy" is to be used as the believer's guidebook "until the day dawn, and the day star arise in your hearts." The world in which we live is shrouded with the darkness of sin, suffering, and sorrow. But true followers of the Lord Jesus have hope in their hearts, the "blessed hope" of the soon coming of Him who said in Revelation 22:16, "I am . . . the bright and morning star." Thousands of years ago, the prophet declared, "There shall come a Star out of Jacob, and a Sceptre shall rise out of Israel, and shall smite the corners of Moab, and destroy all the children of Sheth" (Numbers 24:17). Of course, this is speaking of the Lord Jesus Christ and His return in glory to rule with might and authority in a thousand-year reign of righteousness. Every knee will bow to Him at that time and confess Him as "Lord, to the glory of God the Father" (Philippians 2:11). During this earthly reign of Christ, God's people will rule with Him in perfect bodies, free from sin and physical infirmity. They shall be like Him. What a day that will be when the "Day Star" arises and the shadows flee away! Until that time comes, the unsaved will continue to grope about in the darkness of a confused age; but not the children of God. They have "a more sure word of prophecy" that cannot and will not mislead them for it is the eternal Word of our living God.

The Apostle Peter proceeds to tell us how we may know

the Bible is a "sure word of prophecy." "Knowing this first, that no prophecy of the scripture is of any private interpretation." The word "private" here is often translated "its own." In other words, Scripture is to be compared with Scripture, rather than given its own isolated interpretation or meaning. The Bible is not a collection of writings, but a divinely inspired whole; prophecy is not the various individual writers' inspired reflections, but the truth of God. Oftentimes that which the sacred writer recorded was unknown to him, as far as its meaning was concerned. Job declared, "Therefore have I uttered that I understood not; things too wonderful for me, which I knew not" (Job 42:3). Thus, what God's servants wrote was of God's disclosure and origination, as Peter further adds, "For the prophecy came not in old time by the will of man: but holy men of God spake as they were moved by the Holy Ghost."

It is interesting to note that the only reference to the Holy Spirit in the entire Epistle is in connection with the inspiration of the Scriptures. The Spirit was the agency and "holy men of God" were the agents used to give us the written Word. The Spirit impelled and directed the writers, using their personalities, environmental backgrounds, and education to record the truth.

One thing is certain, if the Holy Spirit guided and directed the holy men of old to write the Scriptures, it is impossible for anyone to try to interpret or understand them apart from the Spirit's influence. The unsaved cannot possibly comprehend the meaning of Scripture. They may read the Bible and even teach it, but they are devoid of spiritual perception or discernment. In 1 Corinthians 2:9-10 Paul makes it clear who is in a position to understand

and know what the Bible teaches: "But as it is written, Eye hath not seen, nor ear heard, neither have entered into the heart of man, the things which God hath prepared for them that love Him. But God hath revealed them unto us by His Spirit: for the Spirit searcheth all things, yea, the deep things of God." For whom has God's Word been written? "For them that love Him!" The unsaved do not love God. If they did, they would believe on Christ, who died for their sins. But until one is converted, he will find the Bible to be a closed book. Paul further tells us in this same chapter that "the natural man receiveth not the things of the Spirit of God: for they are foolishness unto him: neither can he know them, because they are spiritually discerned" (1 Corinthians 2:14).

Of course, if an unsaved person reads the Word of God sincerely, with a desire to find salvation, it is quite certain that the Holy Spirit will unfold the way of life to him. This seems to be implied clearly in Jeremiah 29:13, "And ye shall seek Me, and find Me, when ye shall search for Me with all your heart."

One time a salesman, who was not a Christian but prided himself upon being a model citizen and leading an upright moral life, registered at the Davenport Hotel in Spokane, Washington. The Davenport is one of the finer hotels in the city and is well known for its excellence. One morning, while staying at the hotel, he awoke all out of sorts and the first thing to catch his eye was a Gideon Bible on the stand by his bed. The salesman had an aversion toward Gideon Bibles. He could not bear the sight of one in a hotel room. So he picked it up and with all his strength he threw it across the room, where it lay with its binding broken and its pages crumpled. To get it completely out of sight, he kicked it under the bed.

The salesman spent the morning calling on customers. When he returned to the hotel at noon, in his mail box was a note from the hotel manager requesting him to come to the office. He could not imagine what the manager could want, but nevertheless, he went to the office. After a few minutes of greetings the manager asked, "Don't you like our hotel?"

"Why certainly," replied the salesman, "it's the best hotel in my entire territory."

"Well then, don't you think you should respect our property better?" asked the manager. He reached for the battered Bible, which the housekeeper had brought down to show him. Holding it before the salesman, he said, "Do you think for one minute that we want a guest in our hotel who destroys property in any such shameful way as this? We consider the Gideon Bible as much a part of a room's furnishings as soap and towels. We would never think of running our hotel without Bibles in the rooms. Now, please go to your room, pack up, and get out!"

In a daze, the salesman walked slowly to his room. As he entered, the first thing he noticed was that a new Bible had replaced the one he had ruined. He picked the Bible up gently and sat down while he continued to take mental stock of himself.

"I must be all wet!" he thought, "there must be something to this Book after all. This is one of the finest hotels in the entire country, and the manager tells me that he would no more think of running his hotel without the Bible than he would think of running it without soap and towels; and what's more, he is kicking me out because I kicked the Bible. I guess I had better read it for myself."

He sat down and began thumbing through the pages of the new Bible. Almost immediately the Holy Spirit directed him to passages that reveal man's utter sinfulness and need of the Saviour. As he continued to read, his eyes were opened to the great truth of salvation through Christ. Falling to his knees, he cried out to God in humble repentance. After inviting Christ into his heart, he stood to his feet, a new man in Christ.

Quickly he went to the manager and told him what had happened, apologizing for having behaved so contemptibly. He paid for the damaged Bible and was forgiven, not only by God but also by the hotel manager.

We may be sure, if one approaches God's holy Word humbly and reverently with a desire to know the truth, the Holy Spirit will reveal it. Maybe you are not yet a Christian. Hidden in your heart there are disturbing doubts barricading you from the joy of salvation. Delay no longer, take your Bible and ask the Holy Spirit to unfold the truth to you. It will not be long until you will be thoroughly convinced that you, too, like the innumerable host of redeemed saints, can be eternally saved by believing on the Lord Jesus Christ.

Not only does the Holy Spirit give clear light from the Bible to those seeking salvation, but He faithfully illumines the mind and heart of the believer who daily studies God's truth. In fact, without complete dependence on the Spirit for understanding of the Word, even God's children may become the devil's targets for his shafts of error. The Lord Jesus in foretelling the Spirit's ministry said, "But the Comforter, which is the Holy Ghost, whom the Father will send in My name, He shall teach you all things, and bring all things to your remembrance, whatsoever I have said unto you" (John 14:26). The Holy Spirit who gave the Word must also teach the Word or we shall have no knowledge of its meaning.

Let us also consider the caliber of men God chose to record the Scriptures. Were they educated men? Some were; some were not. Were they wealthy men? Some were; some were not. They were of various ages, from divers walks of life. They differed in many other ways. But there was one outstanding likeness among them all: Peter informs us that they were "holy men." Could there have been any more-needed requisite for those who were chosen to record the Scriptures than that of holiness? If the Holy Spirit elected to work through "holy men" to reveal the Word of God, what kind of individuals must we be if we are to understand the message and the meaning of the Scriptures? Does it sound reasonable that Spirit-filled saints should write the Word while carnal, worldly, defeated Christians are left to read it? It is quite certain that God never intended that such should be the case.

How can we get the most out of this blessed Book which Peter terms "a more sure word of prophecy"? There is only one way—by surrendering our entire selves to God. The Lord Jesus said to the ecclesiastical leaders of his day, "Ye do err, not knowing the scriptures, nor the power of God" (Matthew 22:29). These leaders were confused in their knowledge of the message of the Scriptures because they were not in a position to receive the truth. Knowledge of the Scriptures and the power of God go together. God's power is experienced only through full commitment to the control of the Holy Spirit: "Ye shall receive power, after that the Holy Ghost is come upon you" (Acts 1:8).

If you are one of God's own through Christ, please realize that in the Bible you have God's eternal revelation to mankind, overflowing with precious truths for Spirit-filled hearts. Are you taking the time you should to read and study this wonderful Book? Even more important, are you in a position spiritually to receive the treasures God has for you in His Word? If not, bow before Him at this very moment and surrender completely to His lordship.

If you have not yet come to our Saviour for salvation, let me invite you to come to Him now. You will never regret it. This will be the greatest decision you have ever made. Believe on the Lord Jesus now.

8.

RENUNCIATION

"But there were false prophets also among the people, even as there shall be false teachers among you, who privily shall bring in damnable heresies, even denying the Lord that bought them, and bring upon themselves swift destruction. And many shall follow their pernicious ways; by reason of whom the way of truth shall be evil spoken of. And through covetousness shall they with feigned words make merchandise of you: whose judgment now of a long time lingereth not, and their damnation slumbereth not."—2 Peter 2:1-3

Having concluded chapter one of his second Epistle, which deals with the true prophets of God, "moved by the Holy Ghost," Peter turns next to the false prophets who were causing so much disturbance within the Church. "But there were false prophets also among the people, even as there shall be false teachers among you." We might well wonder how a Church with such a marvelous and miraculous beginning could be tainted with error so soon and so easily. But let us never forget that there is a mighty deceiver sowing the seeds of unbelief and doubt constantly, "Your adversary the devil, as a roaring lion, walketh about, seeking whom he may devour" (1 Peter 5:8). Naturally he does not waste time sowing his seeds of error among the ungodly and unbelieving; they belong to him. He is concerned about those who are proclaiming and living the truth. For this reason, wherever or whenever truth is taught, the devil will appear with his counterfeit.

Paul in his farewell address to the Ephesian elders exhorted them "to feed the church of God"—that is, teach the saints, establish them securely in the truth. For what reason? He tells us in Acts 20:29 and 30: "For I know this, that after my departing shall grievous wolves enter in among you, not sparing the flock. Also of your own selves shall men arise, speaking perverse things, to draw away disciples after them." Paul was well aware of the devil's subtle attempt to destroy the truth. Be assured the evil one is nonetheless crafty in his effort in our day. We must constantly resist him; not in our own strength, but as Peter says in his first Epistle, "Whom resist stedfast *in the faith*" (1 Peter 5:9). It is impossible to resist the devil by human ingenuity or sheer force. With God-given power we must face him in the Lord's strength, armed with the "sword of the Spirit, the Word of God." The truth of God's infallible Word can rout out the enemy and put him to flight.

Peter proceeds to tell us of the strategy frequently used by false teachers in advancing fallacy among the people of God. "Who privily shall bring in damnable heresies." "Privily" as used here means "secretly," with a view to deceive. "Bring in" means literally to "bring in alongside." That is, they bring in error and place it alongside of truth, seeking to cover up their deception.

The untaught, nominal Christian is an easy prey for

this delusive method used by false teachers. Many people who call themselves Christians think that anything that bears the name of God or Christ must surely be all right. Usually they are untaught and spend very little time with their Bibles searching the Scriptures. Consequently, they are wholly incapable of distinguishing between truth and error. Thousands who are now deluded by some of the diabolical cults of our day are those who were at one time in our Sunday schools and churches, but they failed to submit to the claims of Christ as revealed in the Word of God. Thus, when they were confronted with the admixture of truth and error, they did not know the difference. They accepted it, believed it, and now have become slaves to it.

How we need to be mindful of this satanic method of deception being used by scores of cults in our day! Years ago, the Lord Jesus gave us a clear-cut warning that needs to be heeded: "For there shall arise false Christs, and false prophets, and shall shew great signs and wonders; insomuch that, if it were possible, they shall deceive the very elect" (Matthew 24:24). False teachers are no respecters of persons. They are bold enough to thrust their error at God's choice saints, even "the very elect."

Let no fellowship of believers in Christ ever feel that they are beyond attack as far as Satan and error are concerned. While I was the pastor of a church that has never been known as anything other than a strong, orthodox testimony for Christ, the report came to me that one of our Sunday school teachers was teaching some peculiar doctrines. I could hardly believe it, for not only was this young man well liked and respected as one of our church officers, but he had taught his splendid class of young businessmen for a number of years with only the best of reports. In addition to this, he was not a novice in his knowledge of the Scriptures. He was well known as a sincere, faithful student of the Word. Thus, when I heard the report, I said to some of the other officers of the church who had come to me with the problem, "It can't be."

But the following Sunday I discovered that it could be. For then someone came to me with literature that had just been distributed in the classroom. Reading it I found that it was a very cleverly written introductory study to British-Israelism, a system of many grotesque and fanciful interpretations of God's Word. There I held in my hands something I thought could not be. Right under our roof was false teaching, in spite of the fact that from its inception years before, our church had never been known as anything other than a conservative, gospel-preaching witness.

Immediately I called our church board together. We invited the Sunday school teacher in question to meet with us. To our amazement we found that he was steeped in the teachings of British-Israelism. In fact, during the course of that meeting, which ran far into the night, he did his best to try to convince us that the only possible way of truth was that advocated by the British-Israelites. At the conclusion of the meeting, it became necessary to ask him to resign as an officer and a Sunday school teacher. We invited him to continue to attend our services, but until he renounced British-Israelism he was asked not to assume any leadership responsibility in the church.

This experience was a stern warning to all of us who were officers in the church that we must take nothing for granted. Our being an evangelical church was no assurance that Satan would not endeavor to disrupt our fellowship with false teaching. Indeed what Peter wrote years ago is for us today, "There shall be false teachers among you, who privily shall bring in damnable heresies." The "damnable heresies" are literally "destructive heresies" or "heresies of destruction." Not only do they destroy unity and harmony found among true believers, but they entail destruction on all who follow them. Paul mentions this as he writes of the false teachers and their followers in Philippians 3:19, "Whose end is destruction, whose God is their belly, and whose glory is in their shame, who mind earthly things."

It is quite clear from what Peter says that the false teachers he is writing about were unsaved, "Even denying the Lord that bought them, and bring upon themselves swift destruction." Can one deny Christ and still be saved? Peter denied Christ many years before and he was saved. But Peter's denial was not a denial of the fact of the deity of Christ as the Son of God. Peter's plight was one of backsliding—not of apostasy. Backsliding implies a falling back into sin, but not necessarily a falling from grace. The backslider may be restored to fellowship with the Lord by sincere confession. God makes this fact clear in 1 John 1:9, "If we confess our sins, he is faithful and just to forgive us our sins, and to cleanse us from all unrighteousness."

Apostasy, on the other hand, is a deliberate denial and rejection of Christ as the Son of God after having professed Him as Lord. It seems quite obvious, however, that apostates were never truly born again in the beginning. They go through all the motions by making an outward profession but have not sincerely received Christ. God has given them an opportunity to be saved but they have spurned it. This is a serious offense, as we read in Hebrews 6:4-6, "For it is impossible for those who were once enlightened, and have tasted of the heavenly gift, and were made partakers of the Holy Ghost, And have tasted the good word of God, and the powers of the world to come, If they shall fall away, to renew them again unto repentance; seeing they crucify to themselves the Son of God afresh, and put Him to an open shame."

There is no intimation that those of whom the apostle is writing in these verses were ever born again. The Holy Spirit dealt with them. He opened their blinded eyes to the truth. He quickened their understanding by giving them a taste of the truth. But though they may have gone along for a while, even preaching the truth, they were insincere, not truly regenerated by the Holy Spirit. Eventually they turned away from the truth completely. As Peter tells us, they denied "the Lord that bought them." Christ's death, burial, and resurrection became meaningless to them. As a result, they "bring upon themselves swift destruction," that is, they ultimately experience all the horrible consequences of a Christ-rejecting life. There is no hope—"It is impossible . . . to renew them again unto repentance."

Further, in describing the hopelessness of apostasy God says in Hebrews 10:29, "Of how much sorer punishment, suppose ye, shall he be thought worthy, who hath trodden under foot the Son of God, and hath counted the blood of the covenant, wherewith he was sanctified, an unholy thing, and hath done despite unto the Spirit of grace?" Oh, what a tragedy! The apostate might have been saved but he chose heresy rather than truth. The blood of Christ was shed for his sin as well as for the sin of any other unsaved person, but he was more interested in his vain philosophies of humanism than in the inspired truth of God.

The word Peter used for "heresies" refers to self-chosen doctrines rather than those that have emanated from God. In Colossians 2:22-23 Paul speaks of the "commandments and doctrines of men . . . which things have indeed a shew of wisdom in will worship." This is the essence of heresy—"will worship" as opposed to "God worship." But though the "doctrines of men" may ease the troubled conscience of selfish hearts temporarily, their final goal Peter reminds us is "swift destruction."

The false teachers are never without their following. Very often they have a large following, as the apostle says, "*Many* shall follow their pernicious ways." Perhaps you have wondered how the false teachers get so many adherents. It would seem at times that it is far easier to get people to believe error than truth. Peter tells us why. Actually, it is not the false teachers they follow as much as their "pernicious ways." This does not refer especially to the heresies false teachers disseminate but rather the immoral lives they live. Of course, their lives are the result of their teaching. But under most false systems of doctrine, the unsaved can continue on in their sins, with the promise of nothing to fear.

The word used by Peter for "pernicious" means unbridled lust and licentiousness. No wonder the false teachers were so popular. What they taught appealed to man's corrupt and sinful heart. John tells us that "men loved darkness rather than light" (John 3:19). But is the situation any different today? Tell the unsaved that they can continue on in the paths of sin, that they can live for themselves and still go to Heaven. Will not such teaching find many ready supporters? But tell them they must bow to Christ to be saved, that bowing to Christ is more than making a profession of faith, that it is committing one's self completely to God with the forsaking of sin, and the interest will certainly wane. Let us remind ourselves, however, that in spite of what man thinks or teaches, there is only one way to be saved—God's way.

The great tragedy is that many who follow false teachers and their false teaching do so with sincere hearts. Little do they realize that even though they are perfectly sincere in believing what they do, they are sincerely wrong. How often we have heard it said, "It doesn't make any difference what one believes, as long as he is sincere." Sincerity is a factor in salvation, but it is not the determining factor. Sincerity alone has never taken anyone to Heaven; on the other hand, it has sent millions to hell. Sincerity is not a safe guide.

Some years ago, while I was the pastor of a church in Peoria, Illinois, one of the fine Christian women in our church died. She was to be buried the following Monday in Dayton, Ohio, which was about three hundred twenty-five miles from Peoria. Her husband asked if it would be possible for me to conduct the funeral service. I assured him that it could be arranged. I contacted another preacher who consented to speak at our evening service, as my wife and I planned to leave immediately after our Sunday morning worship service, expecting to reach Dayton late that evening.

We left Peoria right after lunch on Sunday. We had only gone twenty-five miles or so when it began to snow. It turned extremely cold and the farther we drove the heavier the snowfall became. Driving became extremely hazardous on the slick, ice-covered highway. Traffic was slowed down to no more than thirty-five miles an hour. The numerous cars and trucks that had already skidded off the highway into the ditch were a constant warning to drive slowly and carefully. As the storm became more severe, road signs and markers were completely covered with ice and snow and were no longer helpful.

About ten o'clock that evening, after driving continuously and steadily so as not to lose any time, we could not understand why we had not reached Indianapolis, which was about two hundred twenty-five miles from Peoria and one hundred miles from Dayton. About five o'clock in the evening we had passed through West Lafayette, Indiana, only sixty miles from Indianapolis. Surely within five hours we should have covered those sixty miles. Stopping at the next service station I asked the attendant how far it was to Indianapolis.

"Oh," he said, "close to two-hundred miles."

"What!" I exclaimed. "How far is it to Peoria?"

"About thirty miles," he replied slowly.

"Which way is it to Peoria?" I asked. He looked at my car and said, "The same way you are headed." Quickly I got in the car, turned around, and off we drove for Dayton. With only a couple hours taken out for needed rest, we reached our destination one hour before the funeral service, which was scheduled for one o'clock Monday afternoon.

My wife and I pondered what had happened. We recalled that at West Lafayette, there had been a detour. Somehow, with the heavy snow and the confusion of a strange city we got turned around. We had no idea we were headed in the wrong direction. We were sincere in thinking we were going in the right direction, but we were sincerely wrong. How easy it is to be sincere in one's thinking and believing, and yet sincerely wrong! My wife and I thought we were going the right way. We were sincere, with good intentions. We knew we were on the right highway, for occasionally we saw a snow-covered marker where the number was not obscured. But in spite of our sincerity, we were wrong.

So often is not the same true in religious matters? Millions of people in our world today have accepted teachings which they sincerely believe. But these teachings are not founded on the Word of God. They present what men think rather than what God says. The Bible declares that "there is a way which seemeth right unto a man, but the end thereof are the ways of death" (Proverbs 14:12). Test your belief! Be sure it is of God. If it is, believe it! Believe it sincerely!

One of the things that disturbed Peter was the effect the false teachers' wicked lives had on the unbelieivng world. Those outside the church would readily sense the hypocrisy within the Church and thus Peter says, "The way of truth shall be evil spoken of." Hypocrisy would be identified with Christians in general, causing unbelievers to consider all Christians as being the same. As a result, they would blaspheme and malign Christians and have no respect for the gospel whatever. Peter foresaw this. Thus in his first Epistle he says, "Having your conversation honest among the Gentiles: that, whereas they speak against you as evildoers, they may by your good works, which they shall behold, glorify God in the day of visitation" (1 Peter 2:12). If God's people are to point lost and dying men and women to Christ, they must not only speak the Word but live the Word. Sound doctrine is best proved by right living.

As is so often the case, we find that the false teachers of which Peter was speaking were not only guilty of lying about God's truth and of living immoral lives, they were also running a racket. They were getting rich quickly while draining their eager followers of their money. Peter writes, "And through covetousness shall they with feigned words make merchandise of you." The poor, deluded followers of the false teachers thought they were being helped. Little did they realize that they were being used as fools for the selfish teachers who were making merchandise of them. Likewise, many who have been duped by the false teaching of our day do not imagine that they are the victims of selfish, money-grabbing, religious racketeers.

Occasionally we hear of false teachers and their methods being exposed. They are comparatively few. Most of them are successful in hiding their sin. But the apostle informs us that the day is coming when not only all will be exposed, but they will receive their just reward—eternal misery, "Whose judgment now of a long time lingereth not, and their damnation slumbereth not." This is to say that the condemnation God has pronounced on false teachers will not be overlooked. Though they are permitted for a season to live in their "pernicious ways" making "merchandise" of their prey, the "swift destruction" will soon come and they will be cast into hell forever. "Be sure your sin will find you out," God says in Numbers 32:23. Indeed it will. No one can handle the Word of God unreasonably and deceitfully without suffering the consequences.

This behooves all of us to ask ourselves: "Is what I believe based upon the clear-cut teachings of the Word of God? Do I know the truth and am I really obeying the truth?" Nothing else will do. The Bible is truth. Its central message is salvation through the Lord Jesus Christ. Do you know Him? Have you received Him into your heart? If not, do so now and then He will guide you into all truth as you prayerfully follow Him.

9.

RETRIBUTION

"For if God spared not the angels that sinned, but cast them down to hell, and delivered them into chains of darkness, to be reserved unto judgment; And spared not the old world, but saved Noah the eighth person, a preacher of righteousness, bringing in the flood upon the world of the ungodly; And turning the cities of Sodom and Gomorrha into ashes condemned them with an overthrow, making them an ensample unto those that after should live ungodly; And delivered just Lot, vexed with the filthy conversation of the wicked: (For that righteous man dwelling among them, in seeing and hearing, vexed his righteous soul from day to day with their unlawful deeds;) The Lord knoweth how to deliver the godly out of temptations, and to reserve the unjust unto the day of judgment to be punished."—2 Peter 2:4-9

In the last verse of our previous study the apostle made it clear that judgment for the false teachers is certain. Though they may deceive many for scores of years, ultimately they must face God and be eternally convicted of their wickedness. The verses above elaborate further on this fact. It is for this reason that I have chosen to give this portion of Scripture the theme of "Retribution." God makes it clear in this passage from historic examples that all sin must be punished, and that no one outside the fold of God can escape judgment.

Three examples of doom are cited by Peter: the fallen angels, the world before the flood, and Sodom and Gomorrha. Of course, there are many more examples of judgment recorded in the Scriptures, but these three should be enough to convince anyone of the impending damnation of the ungodly.

As we proceed in the study of this chapter, you will probably realize its striking similarity to the Epistle of Jude, although when Jude gives his examples of judgment, he says nothing of deliverance. Peter contrasts the judgment of the wicked with the deliverance of the righteous. In two of the three examples he gives of judgment, he stresses the fact that "the Lord knoweth how to deliver the godly out of temptation."

Turning to our first example—that of fallen angels —we are reminded of the fact that regardless of one's position, sin must always be judged. The angels were the highest form of intelligent creatures. This fact, however, did not excuse their disobedience. As to the nature of their sin Peter is silent. Elsewhere in Scripture we recognize their sin was pride. This is a horrible sin, one that God abominates, and yet it is a sin so common even among those who profess to be followers of Jesus Christ.

Probably the most repeated theme in the Bible is the love of God. But God not only loves, He also hates. In Proverbs 6:17-19 God lists seven things He hates. At the top of the list is "a proud look." In Isaiah 5:21 He declares, "Woe unto them that are wise in their own eyes, and prudent in their own sight!" In Proverbs 27:2 He says, "Let another man praise thee, and not thine own mouth; a stranger, and not thine own lips." God hates pride.

Actually, what does any of us have to be proud about? All we possess and all we are is because of the wonderful grace of the Lord Jesus Christ. Physical life, prosperity, health, happiness—are these not all the gifts of God? Could He not bring any of us to the dust in a matter of seconds were it His good pleasure? If for no other reason, we should surrender our hearts and lives fully to Christ because of all He has done for us. We should live out-and-out for Him, reserving nothing for self. Be sure, the closer we get to Him, the farther we shall get from ourselves and the less of pride we shall know.

A little boy was walking down a street in Chicago with his father. They passed a place where a skyscraper was being constructed. Glancing up they saw men at work on a high story.

"Daddy, what are those little boys doing up there so high?" said the child.

"They are not little boys, they are grown men."

"But why do they look so small?"

"Because they are so high."

"Then, Daddy, when they get to Heaven there won't be anything left of them, will there?" How true it is, that the nearer we come to Christ, the smaller we become ourselves. We are so proud and boastful because our experience with the Lord Jesus is so shallow.

In further advancing the theme of "Retribution," Peter reminds us of the judgment that came upon the world in the form of a flood. All of life and civilization was completely destroyed, with the exception of Noah and his seven family members, along with the animals and the fowl that were taken into the ark. For a hundred and twenty years Noah had faithfully proclaimed the message of God prior to the flood. Those to whom he preached refused to listen. They mocked him and laughed at him. They chose to continue in the old paths of sin. Many of the people to whom Noah preached were religious people. There were teachers of religion among them. They refused to listen to the message of truth from the lips of God's servant. Finally, as God had prophesied through the "preacher of righteousness," judgment came. The heavens were opened, the rains fell. The valleys and then the mountain tops were covered with water, and all of life was blotted out. Only those who entered the ark of safety were preserved.

The judgment by means of the flood convinces me of the truth of two verses of Scripture: Ezekiel 18:20 and Romans 10:13. In Ezekiel 18:20 we read, "The soul that sinneth, it shall die." Here God states the fact of His judgment on sin. As surely as all who were outside of the ark in Noah's day perished in their sin, so shall all outside of Christ in our day. Whether they be religious or not, if they have not experienced the redeeming power of Christ, they are lost. But God pleads with all now, as He did with the lost through Noah, saying in the words of Romans 10:13, "For whosoever shall call upon the name of the Lord shall be saved." Have you called on His Name for salvation? I am not asking if you are trying to live a good life, if you belong to a church, if you have been confirmed, if you have been baptised; but have you definitely called on the Lord Jesus Christ and received Him as the Lord of your life?

There have been occasions in my ministry when people, with whom I have talked about receiving Christ, have told me of their Christian heritage, how they were reared in a Christian home with a fine mother and dad. They have tried to use this as a kind of cover-up for their sins. When pressing them to the point I have discovered that down deep in their own hearts they were simply trusting in the goodness of their mother and dad to get them to Heaven. This is not only an absurdity, it is an impossibility. The Bible repeatedly calls for a personal experience with God. In John 3:18 we read, "He that believeth on Him [Christ]is not condemned." This verse does not say, "He that trusts in the faith of his mother or father is not condemned." Salvation is not through parents, even godly ones, but through Christ.

One time while conducting a meeting, D. L. Moody asked all those who needed the Lord and who wished to be prayed for to come forward and kneel or take seats in the front. Among those who came was a pleasant-faced woman. He thought by her looks that she must be a Christian, but she knelt down with the others. Moody said, "You are a Christian, are you not?" She assured him that she had been one for many years.

"Did you understand the invitation?" asked Moody. "I requested that only those who wanted to become Christians come forward." The evangelist recounted that he could never forget the look on her face as she replied, "I have a son who has gotten far away from the Lord. I thought I would take his place today and see if God would not bless him."

All of us can understand the love and concern of this mother's heart to see her boy come to Christ. What parents are not grieved and burdened to see their sons or daughters faltering in the paths of wickedness and sin? But be assured, nowhere in the Bible are we told that a parent, or anyone else for that matter, can make a decision to effect salvation in the heart of another. Each one must make his own decision to receive Christ; otherwise he must suffer the consequences: eternal judgment. For this reason, if you have never yet come to the Lord, God says to you, "Seek ye the Lord while He may be found, call ye upon Him while He is near" (Isaiah 55:6).

You will find Him if you look for Him. You will find Him in creation; you will find Him in His Son; you will find Him in His Word; you will find Him in His Spirit; you will find Him in His promises; you will find Him in His people. Call on Him in prayer; call in the language of the Bible; call upon Him "while He is near."

Peter reminds us next of the appalling and frightful consequences that befell the prosperous cities of Sodom and Gomorrha. The failure of these cities was the result of gross moral impurity. Because of the absence of repentance, with an ambitious desire to continue in the lowest forms of sensuality, these cities were reduced to ashes, judged by God.

Probably when the inhabitants of these two wicked cities finally face their Creator and Judge at the Great White Throne judgment, they will argue that because of so much sin around them, little could be expected of them. But God reminds us that we are not to be the products of our environment; we are to be the products of His grace and love. It is true that a man can rise no higher than his environment. But one who is born of the Spirit of God becomes a new creation in Christ and is enabled by the grace of God to live above the temptations of his environment.

Actually, it is not the environment that makes one either good or bad. Adam and Eve had the best possible environment in the Garden of Eden, but they fell, notwithstanding. It is the heart of man which is deceitful above all things and desperately wicked. The Lord Jesus said in Mark 7:21-23, "For from within, out of the heart of men, proceed evil thoughts, adulteries, fornications, murders, thefts, covetousness, wickedness, deceit, lasciviousness, an evil eye, blasphemy, pride, foolishness: All these evil things come from within, and defile the man." Thank God that Jesus Christ, His Son, cleanseth us from all sin. God who knows the heart purifies it by faith. After one comes to Christ it becomes his responsibility to stock his heart with a good treasure of the Word of God, that he may stand against the evil one, thus overcoming the temptations of his environment.

Peter makes it clear that Lot was able to trust in the Lord, even in the midst of the most appalling conditions. To be sure, Lot was not a victorious believer, but he was a child of God. Lot was "vexed with the filthy conversation of the wicked"; that is, he was tortured and tormented by the licentious behavior of many around him, but he followed the Lord. Like all of us, he had his faults and they were many; but he trusted in the grace of God for deliverance and the Lord did not fail him. Surely, he might have enjoyed greater blessing had he given the Lord first place in his heart. He was saved, but like many followers of the Lord he missed God's best on this earth.

There are many Lots in our day. They know the Lord, of that I am convinced; but in so many cases they are mastered by the world. Lot did little by way of bearing a clearcut testimony for the Lord among his friends and neighbors. In fact, he even failed to be a witness to his own family. It was hard for them to tell whether he belonged to the Lord or to the devil. Cannot the same be said of some professing Christians you may know?

One of the great tragedies of the American Civil War was the death of General Stonewall Jackson. He died on May 2, 1863, through a "mistake." He apparently looked so much like the enemy that his own soldiers, seeking to ambush the Union Army patrol, killed him, thinking he was a Union Army officer. This reminds me of many Christians; they are so like the world that they cannot be truly identified.

God says in 1 John 2:15-17, "Love not the world, neither the things that are in the world. If any man love the world, the love of the Father is not in him. For all that is in the world, the lust of the flesh, and the lust of the eyes, and the pride of life, is not of the Father, but is of the world. And the world passeth away, and the lust thereof: but he that doeth the will of God abideth for ever." These verses make it clear that the child of God is to separate himself from anything that displeases Christ or hinders him from being an effectual witness for Christ.

Alexander Maclaren, a great preacher of a former generation, has written most helpfully concerning the relationship of the believer and the world: "The world conquers me when it succeeds in hindering me from seeing, loving, holding communion with, and serving my God. I conquer it when I lay my hand upon it and force it to help me to get nearer to Him, to get more like Him, to think oftener of Him, to do His will more gladly and more constantly. The one victory over the world is to bend it to serve me in the highest thing—the attainment of a clearer vision of the divine nature, the attainment of a deeper love to God Himself and a more glad consecration and service to Him. That is the victory—when you make the world a ladder to lift you to God. When the world comes between you and God as an obscuring screen, it has conquered you. When the world comes between you and God as a transparent medium, you have conquered it. To win victory is to get it beneath your feet and stand upon it, and reach up thereby to God."

Those of us who are in Christ are called of God to be a separated people, not separated from sinners, but from sin. Even the Lord Jesus ate with publicans and sinners. In Matthew 11:19 we read that he was "a *friend* of publicans and sinners." Our Lord did not always "travel with His own crowd." Very often He was found with the devil's crowd—not to be a part of them and to fellowship in their sins, but to draw them out of their world of iniquity into a world of righteousness that they might find life; and, as we read in John 10:10, "that they might have it more abundantly." Likewise, every child of God is to be in the world but not of it. We are here to point men and women to something better. We cannot possibly do this if we are all tied up with the world and its pursuits. God makes this clear in James 4:4, "Know ye not that the friendship of the world is enmity with God? whosoever therefore will be a friend of the world is the enemy of God." Are you mastered by the world and yet you call yourself a Christian? Come now to the mastery of Christ. Indeed, He can satisfy. He will satisfy. If you are not satisfied it is because you have not committed yourself to Him completely. The fault is not in the provision which has been made, but in the failure to receive the provision.

Our passage in 2 Peter 2 now concludes with two clearcut statements of fact: "The Lord knoweth how to deliver the godly out of temptations," and "The Lord knoweth how to reserve the unjust unto the day of judgment to be punished." Here is truth clearly stated. Let us analyze these facts separately.

First, "The Lord knoweth how to deliver the godly out of temptations." God is never at a loss for means. We cannot deliver ourselves. We have tried scores of times and failed. We have sought to overcome displeasing habits and attitudes but have found this process as hopeless as trying to put new wine into old bottles. Some of us were forced to our knees in our perplexity. We cried unto God for deliverance. We found that what David said in Psalm 34:17 was absolutely true, "The Righteous cry, and the Lord heareth, and delivereth them out of all their troubles." We thought our situation was hopeless; we feared that it might be beyond help. But in 1 Corinthians 10:13 God assured us that this was not the case. He declares, "There hath no temptation taken you but such as is common to man: but God is faithful, who will not suffer you to be tempted above that ye are able; but will with the temptation also make a way to escape, that ye may be able to bear it." By faith we took God at His Word. We found the Word to be true. He did all He said He would.

An orthopedic surgeon, professor in one of the great medical schools of our country, took hold of a young man's leg, which had been fractured in an accident some weeks before. The skilled doctor slapped the boy's leg with rough gestures and said, "It may break again, but you can be sure that the last place it will ever break is where it broke before because the calcification around that fracture has increased the strength of the bone tremendously."

As God performs miracles in the healing of the body, so He performs miracles in the healing of the soul. After one comes to Christ, he discovers that though he was utterly weak and helpless in facing particular temptations, now he is strong. The devil may attack frequently, but the Lord never fails to give the victory if we trust Him for it.

Should you need His help at this moment, it avails for you. Maybe you are a child of God, and you are facing some test of life; trust the Lord; lean on Him; believe Him; take your entire burden to Him.

On the other hand, perhaps you are not a child of God. Your inner resources are useless in coping with the problems of the complex life we face today. You need Christ in your heart. Turn to Him this very moment. You have no time to lose, for God makes it clear that the soul, following physical death, must go to eternal judgment.

This is the other fact of 2 Peter 2:9, "The Lord knoweth how to reserve the unjust unto the day of judgment to be punished." As the angels of God were cast down to hell and delivered into the chains of darkness to be reserved unto judgment because of their sins, so must you be if you do not come to Christ. As God brought judgment by means of a flood to all of civilization because of rebellious hearts, so He must bring judgment on you if you refuse to come to Christ. As He turned the cities of Sodom and Gomorrha into ashes because of prevailing immorality, so He must judge you if you do not trust in the Lord Jesus Christ. All sin must be judged.

The choice is yours. Either you can escape judgment by believing on Christ who was judged for all believing sinners on the cross or you must suffer your own judgment in the fires of eternal hell. Which will you accept? If you have not done so already, I trust that you will believe on the Lord Jesus Christ; and like Noah in the ark and the scores of other saints named in the Word of God, be forever delivered from the judgment of God. Do not spurn God's wonderful offer of salvation. Believe on Christ now.

I have read of a Duxbury, Massachusetts, man who refused to pay one-cent postage due on a letter he received. The letter was returned to the Plymouth dead-letter office. Postmaster William Goodwin disclosed that when the letter was opened he found a $450 check enclosed. It was returned immediately to the sender in Boston.

Before you criticize the man who refused to pay one cent for the check-laden letter, be sure you have answered this question: "Have I received the message on which nothing is due and which offers me that which money cannot buy and works cannot secure, namely, Eternal Life?" Here is the message: "For God so loved the world, that He gave His only begotten Son, that whosoever believeth in

Him should not perish, but have everlasting life" (John 3:16). Is this priceless message but a dead letter to you— to be sent back to the sender, the Lord Jesus Christ?

Evidently the man who refused to pay the one cent due on the business letter did not know that it contained the $450 check. We can be even more charitable and say it was possible the man did not have a cent with which to pay the postage due on the letter. It is quite possible that he will receive the check later, for the sender may readdress it to him with the proper amount of postage on it.

But can it be said of you that you do not know that John 3:16 contains an offer of everlasting life and an escape from judgment? Even if you are without one cent in money, you may still receive the message and enjoy the life it offers, for it is without cost to you. The Lord Jesus paid the price by His death and resurrection, hence He can make such a bona fide offer. Will you reconsider the matter? Please realize the truth of Christ's sacrifice for you and give God the response He deserves by receiving Christ into your heart.

10.

REPUTATION

"But chiefly them that walk after the flesh in the lust of uncleanness, and despise government. Presumptuous are they, selfwilled, they are not afraid to speak evil of dignities. Whereas angels, which are greater in power and might, bring not railing accusation against them before the Lord. But these, as natural brute beasts, made to be taken and destroyed, speak evil of the things that they understand not; and shall utterly perish in their own corruption; And shall receive the reward of unrighteousness, as they that count it pleasure to riot in the day time. Spots they are and blemishes, sporting themselves with their own deceivings while they feast with you; Having eyes full of adultery, and that cannot cease from sin; beguiling unstable souls: an heart they have exercised with covetous practices; cursed children."—2 Peter 2:10-14

Having made it clear that judgment for false teachers is certain, Peter proceeds to expose the reputation of the false teachers. With clarity he paints a true picture of these ungodly men who were seeking to destroy the faith of the saints.

He begins by saying that they "walk after the flesh in

the lust of uncleanness." Their god was lust and their guide was the flesh. As used here, "flesh" refers to the depraved nature of man. Paul said of the flesh in Romans 7:18, "For I know that in me (that is, in my flesh,) dwelleth no good thing." The flesh cannot obey God. Thus Paul tells us in Romans 8:8, "So then they that are in the flesh cannot please God." As long as one refuses to submit to the Lordship of Christ and be saved he is still in the flesh and controlled by the flesh. In such a state, it is impossible for him to have favor with God. The only remedy for this condition is to believe on the Lord Jesus Christ.

Without Christ, man is unable to control or restrain himself. Dominated by the flesh, he is an easy prey for lust and uncleanness. At the root of his sinful and wicked deeds is a corrupt and unregenerate heart. In Proverbs 6:18 God speaks of the "heart that deviseth wicked imaginations." This descriptive statement from the Scriptures clearly portrays the condition of the unregenerate, outside the fold of God, whose hearts have never been washed by the blood of Christ.

Peter goes on to tell us that not only are the false teachers controlled and guided by the flesh but they "despise government." This does not refer to political government but rather to the divine control of the soul. In other words, they despise even the thought of submission to Christ. As a result of this, Peter says, they are "presumptuous"; literally, "daring." Not only are they daring in their ridicule of the Lordship of Christ but they are fearless in their accusations of God's servants; "they are not afraid to speak evil of dignities." The reason for all of this is that they are "self-willed." They are motivated by the desire to live for self rather than for God. They hate the Lord but they love themselves. Everything they do or say must in some way result in profit for self. This is the absolute opposite of what it means to be a Christian.

One who is truly born again should be dead to self and mastered by Christ. It is quite obvious that many who think they are saved have never yet experienced the marvelous grace of God. How do we know? The self-life is a dead giveaway. Rather than being mastered by Christ, they are dominated by self. Like the false teachers of Peter's day, they are self-willed rather than Christ-controlled. Let us be reminded, however, that there can be no peace or happiness whatsoever in the self-willed life. Until one turns himself over to Christ completely, he will never know real and lasting satisfaction. The moment one commits himself to Christ, the Saviour takes control and blessedness is the result.

Every student pilot is taught that any bad flying maneuver may end up in a spin. Consequently, one of the first things he must learn is how to recover from a spin. A young pilot tells of the time when his instructor told him that he had come to that place in his training where it was now essential to learn how to recover from a spin. Standing by the plane the instructor explained it all perfectly. Then he said, "Now let us go up and try it." So they climbed steadily upwards over an unpopulated area until 12,000 feet registered on the altimeter.

Going into a spin was easy, just a matter of easing the control column back and then kicking on full rudder. But when the instructor told the student to "recover," that was a different story. The earth was coming up to meet them at 6,000 feet a minute and the plane was shuddering as they spun round and round.

In those few seconds the sweat poured off the young student as he vainly fumbled with the controls, obviously doing everything wrong, until a voice quietly spoke saying, "All right, I've got 'er." Oh, the relief of that voice, as the student handed over the controls. In an instant they were flying on the level again.

Does this not furnish us with a true picture of many persons whose lives are out of control, hurtling toward a lost eternity? There is nothing they can do to save themselves. But through the grace of God they can give up their struggling and hand over the controls to the Lord Jesus Christ. It is as simple as that. If you are not saved and if you are willing to give up your feeble fumbling and ask the Lord Jesus to come into your life and take control, you may be assured that He will come in. He says clearly in His Word in Revelation 3:20: "Behold, I stand at the door, and knock: if any man hear My voice, and open the door, I will come in to him, and will sup with him, and he with Me." When He comes in, the self-life can be transcended by the Christ-life. Do you want the blessedness, the contentment, the joy God has promised in His Word? Then come to Christ, believe on Him!

Peter next enlarges upon the statement he made concerning the presumptuous and daring nature of the false teachers. They were so filled with pride and self-glory that they were profane and vile in their speech toward God. Not only did they openly rebel against Him and His majesty, but also against angelic beings. In addition to this, they were spreading lies about the apostles and pastors, claiming that they were scattering error and that their teachings were of the devil. Indeed the false teachers were on dangerous ground, for God has said in Psalm 105:15, "Touch not Mine anointed, and do My prophets no harm." Here is a serious warning. We must be careful about what we say concerning those whom God has ordained and chosen to be His undershepherds in the Church of Christ. Peter tells us that even the angels, "which are greater in power and might," would not dare accuse God's servants before the Lord. If the angels of God would not consider being guilty of such a thing, who are we to assume such liberty in trespassing the commandment of God in this respect?

The reason the false teachers spoke and acted as they did was very simple. Peter describes them as "natural brute beasts, made to be taken and destroyed." They were like animals, living wholly for the flesh, born to die with no hope beyond the grave. Unlike animals, however, they had eternity to face without God. No man is merely an animal; he may be like an animal in his manner of life, but in reality he is a soul in need of redemption.

The false teachers "speak evil of dignities," Peter says, because "they understand not." That is, they lack spiritual wisdom and perception. Actually, they were devoid of understanding; not because they did not know the truth, but because they refused to submit to the truth. They had closed their minds to God. Though they had heard the gospel and knew God's way of salvation, they chose to believe lies. As a result, God says that they "shall utterly perish in their own corruption; and shall receive the reward of unrighteousness, as they that count it pleasure to riot in the daytime." False teachers must suffer eternal judgment, not because they are false teachers, but because they reject Christ. "The reward of unrighteousness," of course, is eternal separation from God. Though the body returns to dust, the soul will go immediately to hell because of the refusal to believe on the Lord Jesus Christ.

In a previous chapter mention was made of rewards for faithful believers. The Bible not only speaks of the reward of righteousness but also, as we see here, "the reward of unrighteousness." God says in Isaiah 3:11, "Woe unto the wicked! it shall be ill with him: for the reward of his hands shall be given him." What is that reward? Psalm 9:17 gives the answer—"The wicked shall be turned into hell." I have heard some say they are not afraid of hell; they are willing to be sent to this place. Be assured if they knew what hell is like they would repent of their sins in seconds.

The Bible teaches that hell is a place not only of torment, but of *eternal* torment. Jesus in speaking of the death of the wicked in Matthew 25:41 said, "Then shall he say also unto them on the left hand, Depart from Me, ye cursed, into everlasting fire, prepared for the devil and his angels." Also in Matthew 25:46 He said, "And these shall go away into everlasting punishment: but the righteous into life eternal." If the sinner were to die and cease to be, that would be terrible. Missing the glories of God's eternal Heaven would be sad indeed. But hell is more than ceasing to be. Hell, the Bible teaches, is a place of eternal torment. This means that the wicked, the ungodly, and the Christ-rejectors will be there, eternally tormented for their sins.

But somebody says, "I don't believe a God of love would ever send His children to hell." You are absolutely correct. God never prepared hell for His children. In Matthew 25:41 we saw that hell was prepared for "the devil and his angels." God doesn't want anyone to go to hell. Men and women are in hell by choice or because they do not know the truth. We read in 2 Peter 3:9 that God is "not willing that any should perish, but that all should come to repentance." That is why God gave the best He had, His only beloved Son who left the glories of Heaven to come to the shame of this earth to die on the cross of Calvary that He might save you and me from the horrors of hell. No, hell was never prepared for you. Heaven was prepared for you.

The question you need to answer is, "Are you a child of God? Are you ready for Heaven?" You are a child of God only if you have come to Christ and believed on Him. If you have not received Christ into your life, you are not His child. If you are not His child, it doesn't make any difference that you may be a good man, a moral man, a benevolent man; you are still destined to hell until you repent and trust in Christ for salvation.

When Jesus spoke of the rich man and Lazarus in Luke 16, He said nothing against the rich man's morals. There is no intimation that the rich man was covetous, nor do we have any reason to believe he was an adulterer, a murderer, a gambler, or a drunkard. His problem was like that of everyone outside of Christ. He had a sinful heart that had not been redeemed. His worst problem was on the inside, not the outside. God says in 1 Samuel 16:7, "The Lord seeth not as man seeth; for man looketh on the outward appearance, but the Lord looketh on the heart."

Peter has more to say about the reputation of the false teachers: "Spots they are and blemishes, sporting themselves with their own deceivings while they feast with you." This is as much as to say that they were hypocrites. They called themselves Christians. They worshiped with the saints, but they were deceiving themselves. They were like those of whom Jesus spoke in Matthew 15:8, "This people draweth nigh unto Me with their mouth, and honoureth Me with their lips; but their heart is far from Me."

Regrettably, the churches of our day are still plagued with hypocrites. They are "spots" and "blemishes" within our congregations. It is sad but true that most of the criticism coming from the worldly and ungodly is not the result of their observation of sincere believers in Christ, but of the hypocrites.

C. H. Spurgeon used to tell the story of the fruitgrower who invited a friend to visit his orchard to taste his apples. Regardless of many invitations, the friend did not come. At last the fruitgrower said, "I suppose you think my apples are no good, so you won't even come and try them."

"Well, to tell the truth," said his friend, "I have tasted them. As I went along the road I picked one up that fell over the fence, and I have never tasted anything so sour in all my life. After eating that apple, I have decided I don't want any more of your fruit."

"Oh," replied the fruitgrower, "those apples around the outside of the orchard are for the special benefit of the children. I went miles to select the sourest kind of apples to plant all around the orchard so the children might give them up as not worth while stealing. But if you will come inside, you will find that we grow a very different quality there, sweet as honey."

Certainly we have hypocrites in the church. This fact cannot be denied. As long as we are on this side of Heaven, we shall always have hypocrites in the church. But if you are staying away from fellowship with the people of God because of the hypocrites, may I invite you to come on inside and you will see scores of men and women who love God and who are, by His grace, seeking to give Him first place in their lives.

While we are thinking of the hypocrite, it might be a good time for all of us to allow God to examine our own hearts. It is so easy to judge our neighbor as the hypocrite. Are there inconsistencies in your life? Are you guilty of little hypocrisies that God hates? Following the Lord is more than faithful church attendance, diligent Bible reading, and routine habits of prayer. Not only is it requisite that believers love the Lord, but as Christ said in Matthew 22:39, it is loving "thy neighbour as thyself." To love one's neighbor as himself involves equitable and fair dealings with him at all times. God says in 2 Corinthians 8:21, "Providing for honest things, not only in the sight of the Lord, but also in the sight of men." Most hypocrites cannot be distinguished from true believers when they are in church on Sunday; but it is Monday that reveals the difference, for then they are deceitful, dishonest, and unreliable.

A Christian woman sold her house and bought another next to the sister of the woman to whom she sold. The Christian tried to witness to her new neighbor but there was no interest. She tried several times again but was brushed aside each time. One day she frankly asked her neighbor if she didn't care about her soul. The neighbor replied, "Please don't talk any more about religion to me. You sold a house to my sister that you knew very well had many things wrong. We know there were some things over which you had no control, but you lied to her about other things. My sister and I are not Christians, but we certainly wouldn't do what you did. I will be happy to listen to you but only after you have cared for your false claims." The professing Christian was convicted. She realized that this was all too true. She made restitution, but even so, she was never able to get very far in winning her neighbor to Christ.

What about us? Can it be said that we are "spots and blemishes," not only to the church to which we belong but to the cause of Christ? "Let us lay aside every weight, and the sin which doth so easily beset us, and let us run with patience the race that is set before us, Looking unto Jesus the author and finisher of our faith; who for the joy that was set before Him endured the cross, despising the shame, and is set down at the right hand of the throne of God" (Hebrews 12:1-2).

In the concluding verse of our present study Peter lists four more characteristics in describing the reputation of the hypocritical false teachers. "Having eyes full of adultery." Does this not remind us of the words of our Lord in Matthew 5:28: "Whosoever looketh on a woman to lust after her hath committed adultery with her already in his heart." How important that God's people learn to let Him control their eyes. Job said, "I made a covenant with mine eyes; why then should I think upon a maid?" (Job 31:1) The unredeemed man has no control over his eyes as far as lust is concerned, but the child of God has.

In addition to this Peter informs us that the unsaved "cannot cease from sin." Let us not boast of our own moral goodness, for we have none. Paul declared in Romans 7:21, "I find then a law, that, when I would do good, evil is present with me." Here is an inexorable law. The sinful flesh of mankind can desire nothing else than evil. But the redeeming power of Christ can transform his heart so that even though in despair he says with Paul, "O wretched man that I am! who shall deliver me from the body of this death?" He can further say, "I thank God through Jesus Christ our Lord" (Romans 7:24-25).

The sinner is never content to satisfy his own lusts; he seeks always to drag others into his guilt by "beguiling unstable souls." Likewise, the false teacher is not satisfied to embrace his own views; he desires to involve others in his errors.

Finally, Peter makes it clear that, as is the case with all unbelievers, the real problem of the false teachers is a matter of the heart, "an heart they have exercised with covetous practices." It is impossible for good to come out of an evil heart. Thus the false teachers are condemned forever —"cursed children."

How is your heart before God? Are you truly saved? Do you know the Lord? If so, God has given you a new heart, for He promises in Ezekiel 36:26, "A new heart also will I give you, and a new spirit will I put within you: and I will take away the stony heart out of your flesh, and I will give you an heart of flesh." If you need a new heart today,

God is ready and willing to answer your prayer if you will call on the Lord Jesus Christ for salvation. Remember, God looks most where man looks least—at the heart.

A young man, who was a photographer by profession, and who specialized in what are known as close-ups, traveled to another locality on business. On arriving at his destination he visited the leading photographer of the district, who was a staunch follower of the Lord Jesus Christ. When their more mundane affairs were concluded, the Christian said to the young man: "You specialize in close-ups, do you not? Have you ever seen a close-up of your own heart?" And, to his visitor's astonishment he pulled out a copy of the New Testament and read to him Romans 3:10-18, which portrays the utter sinfulness and worthlessness of the heart of man. The incident proved to be the beginning of a Spirit-wrought conviction of need on the part of the young man, leading him ultimately to a saving knowledge of Christ as his Saviour and Lord.

Praise God, though the heart is black with the stains of sin, "the blood of Jesus Christ His Son cleanseth us from all sin" (1 John 1:7). Have you experienced this marvelous cleansing? If not, bow and receive Christ at this very moment. He will receive you if you will come to Him.

11.

REBELLION

"Which have forsaken the right way, and are gone astray, following the way of Balaam the son of Bosor, who loved the wages of unrighteousness; But was rebuked for his iniquity: the dumb ass speaking with man's voice forbad the madness of the prophet."—2 Peter 2:15-16

Peter begins this portion of our study by telling us that the false teachers had "forsaken the right way." They were not ignorant of the truth. It had been their privilege to know God's message, but after appearing to be receiving and believing it they turned away from it. This is rebellion! Such action is a serious offense in the eyes of God. What could be worse than to have the understanding opened to the message of life and then to forsake the truth? Small wonder that the rebellious heart is a sorrowful heart.

The false teachers of whom Peter speaks remind me of Judas. Here was a man who could have been a mighty instrument of power and usefulness for God. He knew the truth, having heard it again and again from the lips of our blessed Lord. Daily he walked in the presence of Christ, eating with Him, conversing with Him, and working with Him. But like the foolish men of our text, Judas forsook Christ.

As I consider Judas' failure, I am reminded of many like him who are comfortably seated in their church pews every Sunday. They know the truth, having heard it week after week, year in and year out. They know how to be saved. Repeatedly they have heard the gospel presented, but as yet they have done nothing about it. They *say* they believe, but their lives prove that they do not. Theirs has been merely a mental acceptance of Christ, while their sinful hearts are still controlled by the devil. Of them the Lord Jesus could say, "And ye will not come to Me, that ye might have life" (John 5:40). What a serious and sad state of affairs, to know the truth and yet to refuse to come to the truth. Few men realize the urgency of getting right with God immediately. If they did, we should see them on every hand, crying aloud to God in repentance. In contrast, however, we see them living for self, carelessly ignoring the claims of Christ on their soul.

If it should be that you are of this class, may I solicit your consideration of something of extreme importance: Can you tell me who can present a satisfactory explanation of the phenomena of physical life? In describing the working mechanism of the human frame the physiologist says, "This muscle moves because it is pulled by another, and the other muscle moves because it is awakened by a certain nerve." Pressing him for an answer, you ask why all this continues and he will tell you, "Because the heart beats."

Going deeper you ask why the heart beats. The physiologist has gone the limit; he is through. He can provide no further answer.

But there is an answer to that question. The heart beats because God moves the heart. There is not a heart beating in the world that does not compress and dilate every second because of the touch of God. This being true, how frightful is the position of one who lives in open rebellion to the One who must move the heart every second. If God were to withhold His finger from the heart of any of us, within seconds we would lie cold and silent. The heartbeat is life, the pause between the heartbeats is death. Every time the heart pauses, it puts the silent question to the Giver of Life, "May I go on?" If it is God's desire that life continue, He says, "Go on." The lease on life is renewed, not every year, not every month, not every week, not every day, but every second. Through the mercy and providence of God we have the sovereign renewal of life every second. God could say to any one of us at any time, "Be still," and the heart would beat for the last time.

Let us not try to side-step reality. Death is inescapable. One day soon the heart of every man will respond to the voice of God, "Be silent." Suppose God were to speak to your heart within the next minute saying, "Cease from labor. Your task is done." Where would you go? Would you meet God or be separated from Him forever? Remember, knowing the truth is not enough. You must believe the truth. You must be reborn by believing on the Lord Jesus Christ.

For fear that you have been one of those who have heard the gospel time and time again but have not submitted yourself to the Lord Jesus Christ, I beseech you to consider the Word of God as it is found in Hebrews 2:1-3: "Therefore we ought to give the more earnest heed to the things which we have heard, lest at any time we should let them slip. For if the word spoken by angels was stedfast, and every transgression and disobedience received a just recompence of reward; How shall we escape, if we neglect so great salvation?" Have you heard the Word but neglected to come to Christ? You are guilty of rebellion. The price of continued rebellion is eternal judgment, but the reward of the acceptance of Christ is eternal life. Do not procrastinate, do not delay any longer. To you God says, "Behold, now is the accepted time; behold, now is the day of salvation" (2 Corinthians 6:2). It is a solemn thing to say "tomorrow" when God says "today."

A doctor said in an article in *Christian Victory* magazine: "Some time ago we saw a man in our office who on examination was found to have an early cancer of the throat. He refused to accept our diagnosis and refused to see another doctor. Some few months later we saw him again and there was evidence that the malignant growth was spreading. Again the patient was adamant, refusing to accept the diagnosis and saying he knew of a sure cure for his trouble. About a month later he again appeared in our office and almost hysterically said he was well, that he had no pain and he knew he was cured. Some six weeks later we read in the paper of his death."

Those who deny the deadly nature of the sin-sickness with which all of us have been afflicted are as ridiculously obstinate. Wise indeed are they who admit that they are sick of soul, go to the Great Physician for salvation, and accept His beloved Son as the perfect panacea for all their ills of heart and soul.

Have you sincerely invited Christ to come into your life or is your so-called relationship to God merely a surface experience? Be assured your chances for getting right with the Lord may soon be past. God says in Genesis 6:3, "My spirit shall not always strive with man." God is pleading with you at this very moment to come to Him before it is too late. Death may be nearer than you think. After death there are no further opportunities to receive Christ.

In Albany, New York, a rabbi performed a "black wedding" recently, following an ancient, eastern European tradition. A young Jewish couple, Norman Saltzburg and Johanne Wohl, were killed in an automobile accident on the day their engagement was to have been announced. The parents requested the rabbi to marry the couple. The two coffins were placed side by side and the rabbi read the Hebrew marriage service, omitting all references to life, and placed the ring on the girl's finger. A copy of the marriage writ was put in the girl's casket.

Those who know the gospel realize how hopeless this ceremony really was. For the Lord has told us that there is no marriage or giving in marriage after this life. The incident, however, can teach us that some day certain things will be too late; the most important of which is the receiving of Jesus Christ as Saviour and Lord. There are some things that should be done immediately, and this is one of them. Time is passing quickly. God says in Psalm 144:4, "Man is like to vanity: his days are as a shadow that passeth away."

Not only did the false teachers know the truth and forsake the truth; we notice that they departed from the truth for something else. Peter tells us that they "are gone astray, following the way of Balaam, the son of Bosor, who loved the wages of unrighteousness." Balaam was the hireling prophet who commercialized his gift. Balaam was more concerned about money than about the will of God. The false teachers of whom Peter speaks were guilty of the same error. They were in the church for the money they could get out of it. They loved money more than the Lord. Doubtless, this was the evil that caused Demas' downfall. Paul says of him in 2 Timothy 4:10, "Demas hath forsaken me, having loved this present world."

Many in our churches today are turning their faces from God to follow the course of the world. They are trying to serve God and gold. The Bible says in Matthew 6:24, "no man can serve two masters: for either he will hate the one, and love the other; or else he will hold to the one, and despise the other. Ye cannot serve God and mammon." Frequently when one tries to serve both God and mammon, he ends up serving mammon only. Money usually gets the better of him.

In 1 Timothy 6:10 God says, "the love of money is the root of all evil." Indeed it is, including the worst evil, that of leading men to sell their Saviour with the same covetous spirit which prompted Judas to ask the envious churchmen in Jerusalem, "What will ye give me, and I will deliver Him unto you?" (Matthew 26:15). Judas proceeded to betray his Lord for only $16.50 in our currency. Some in our churches have sold the Son of God for far less. They have left the church to join organizations which they thought would open their way to more money or greater success. Too often, like Judas who threw the thirty pieces of silver into the sanctuary and then hanged himself, they have lost both gold and God. Others have stopped attending services because certain church members did not trade with them; because the preacher had too much to say about money and missions; or because it was hard to reconcile the message of the church with their methods of making money. For a dozen other selfish reasons they have sought to put cash before Christ. But as of old our Saviour warns, "For what shall it profit a man, if he shall gain the whole world, and lose his own soul? Or what shall a man give in exchange for his soul?" (Mark 8:36,37) Have you sacrificed your soul for a few paltry dollars? Are you living only for a bank account? It is far better to have a bank in Heaven than to have heaven in a bank.

There were two farmers who lived close to each other. One of them worked hard, but he had no money laid away in the bank. During the years he used all his money to help others. He never turned a poor man away from his door. He gave his four children the best education he could: one became a minister, two became teachers, one became a civil engineer. He always shared his home with others: some children who were left as orphans when a friend died; his wife's crippled niece; a little boy he had rescued from the slums of the city. He did all this because he was a true follower of Christ and loved the Lord with all his heart. As the result of this farmer's sacrificial life for Christ, God honored him and prospered his farm. When the farmer died he did not leave his wealth; rather he went to it, for he had faithfully laid up mansions in the sky, treasure that only the kind of life he lived could produce.

Near him lived the other farmer. He was mean and selfish. This farmer was heard to say, "So my neighbor is dead. He died without a penny in the bank. Look at me. I started with nothing and now I own all the broad fields clear down to the creek. When my wife and I started to keep house, I got this iron savings bank. Every penny we could save went into its jaws. Other people ate meat; we ate molasses. Other wives wore silk; my wife wore calico. Other men sent their boys and girls away to school; I taught mine to work. I have wasted no money on churches or people. I am worth a hundred thousand dollars."

The latter farmer lived for himself. He saved all for himself and gave to no one. In God's sight he was a pauper. So are all who lay up treasures for themselves and are not rich toward God. But for the child of God who lives sacrificially, the Lord says, in Proverbs 11:25, "The liberal soul shall be made fat: and he that watereth shall be watered also himself." The sacrificial heart will never want for any good thing. God will provide for and care for His own.

How many in our day are being deceived by the false god of mammon! Even God's dear people—those that have been born of the Spirit—are not free from the temptation to be covetous and selfish. The only satisfactory way to hold earthly possessions is to hold them as God's stewards. Better a little held in this way than great riches any other way.

Whether we serve the Lord in an office, store, factory, or

out on the mission field, we should cultivate the habit of giving part of our income to some definite Christian work. A good way to begin is with the tithe. God says in Malachi 3:10: "Bring ye all the tithes into the storehouse, that there may be meat in Mine house, and prove Me now herewith, saith the Lord of hosts, if I will not open you the windows of heaven, and pour you out a blessing, that there shall not be room enough to receive it."

Though we begin with the tithe, let us not stop with a tenth. As God blesses you, keep growing in grace by honoring the Lord with more than the tithe. One may be a tither, but this does not necessarily mean that he is of a gracious and generous spirit. It is possible to tithe merely out of obligation or duty, or perhaps to be well spoken of by others. There are even mean and penurious men who are tithers. They bargain with the Lord about whether they should take out their taxes before they give their tithes, or whether they should first pay their rent or office expenses. Truly, "the letter killeth, but the spirit giveth life" (2 Corinthians 3:6). The tithe is the letter. Stewardship is the spirit. God's Word makes it clear that we should not give less than the tithe, but those who have been saved by the grace of the Lord Jesus Christ should give much more. Even our Federal government makes an allowance for giving as much as thirty per cent and gives tax exemption on that basis.

In one of our large cities a prominent Christian businessman was driving a visiting Bible teacher around the city, showing him some of the beauty spots. Their conversation turned toward giving to the Lord. The businessman gave his testimony of God's marvelous provision in his life. He said, "When I got my first job I was getting only thirty dollars a month, but I had made up my mind to begin right. I gave a tenth to the church. God prospered me and soon my wife and I decided we could give more, and we began giving fifteen per cent. Now I give twenty per cent and the more I give, the more God blesses."

That last statement is so true, "The more I give the more God blesses." Many of the Lord's people do not know this because they are not giving to the Lord sacrificially. They have not yet come into the reality of the truth spoken by our Lord: "It is more blessed to give than to receive" (Acts 20:35).

A minister in Texas, doing his pastoral round, arrived at a poor Mexican home where a younger member of the family had infantile paralysis. When he left the house, an older boy was stroking one of the shiny fenders of the minister's new car. Saying that he thought it was beautiful, the boy asked, "Where did you get it?"

"Well, Sonny," explained the minister, "I am just a preacher and don't make much money and, of course, could not afford to buy such an expensive automobile. But I have a brother who lives in Dallas who has made a fortune out of oil, and my brother gave me this automobile." The boy's reaction was most interesting. He did not say, "I wish I had a brother like that." Looking up at the minister and speaking from his heart he said, "My, I wish I could be a brother like that."

Here is the spirit that ought to be in the heart of every true servant of the Lord. Our ambition should be not how much can I get, but how much can I give? Oh, child of God, do not be deceived by the wicked one. Get victory over selfishness, consecrate your possessions to God and give to Him accordingly. "Honour the Lord with thy substance, and with the firstfruits of all thine increase" (Proverbs 3:9). Then you will reap the promised blessing: "So shall thy barns be filled with plenty, and thy presses shall burst out with new wine" (Proverbs 3:10). Give according to your income, lest God make your income according to your giving. Fall in love with Christ today. Recognize all that you have as a trust from Him to be used for His glory.

Poor old Balaam failed to get the victory over his selfishness. He forsook the way of the Lord and went astray because of his love for money. God tried to help him, even causing the dumb ass on which he rode to speak like a man. One would think such an unusual phenomenon would cause even the most rebellious to come to his senses, but not Balaam. He was bound by his sin. The sinful heart is always a rebellious heart with no ear for the voice of God.

Could it be, Christian, that God has been speaking to you in some manner during the past days or weeks? In His great love and patient kindness He has sought to direct you into the paths of greatest usefulness for Him. Possibly you, at some time, have gone astray from the road of God's best. Since that hour it seems as though everything has gone wrong. God has sought to speak, but you have failed to listen. Will you at this moment let Him have His perfect way? God's will for your life is the only way of blessedness and happiness. There are so many unhappy and miserable Christians. Why? They are refusing to permit God to run their lives. Nothing can banish joy quicker than planning and promoting one's own interest, rather than following the leading of the Lord.

Our churches are suffering from the tragic effects of so many on the rolls who are not in God's will; consequently they are miserable and disatisfied. One of the most effective ways for a church to make an impact on its community is to send forth a happy band of radiant, victorious Christians into the offices, shops, schools, and homes—Christians who really know how to praise the Lord. Before the unsaved will be inclined to heed our invitations to come to Christ, we must give evidence that our hearts are overflowing with gratitude to God for His abundant mercies.

A high-class restaurant in a great city employed a half dozen men, down-and-outers, hungry and emaciated in appearance, to carry signs on a crowded street to advertise its wonderful meals. Think of it, famished derelicts advertising the best dinners. It would be funny were it not so tragic. Yet something like that is happening in many of our churches every day. Men and women minus the joy of the Lord, with long faces and the corners of their mouths turned down, are the advertisements we are producing for the Lord Jesus Christ, who is supposed to satisfy empty hearts. Our Saviour said in John 15:11, "These things have I spoken unto you, that My joy might remain in you, and that your joy might be full." Do you know the fullness of the joy of the Lord? If not, it is because somehow, somewhere, there is rebellion in your heart. Go to your knees in prayer. Ask God to remove the obstacles that you may seek His will in all things, and, as a result, experience His overflowing joy.

It is possible that you may not be a child of God. You

thought you were a Christian, but you cannot truly say that you love Christ and want Him to be the Lord of your life. Rebel no longer against God's wonderful grace. He gave His best for you; give yourself to Him. Receive God's wonderful salvation by believing on Jesus, His Son. You may be sure He will receive you if you will but turn to Him.

12.

REASSERTION

"These are wells without water, clouds that are carried with a tempest; to whom the mist of darkness is reserved for ever. For when they speak great swelling words of vanity, they allure through the lusts of the flesh, through much wantonness, those that were clean escaped from them who live in error. While they promise them liberty, they themselves are the servants of corruption: for of whom a man is overcome, of the same is he brought in bondage."—2 Peter 2:17-19

Peter reasserts his convictions about the wicked lives and the vain philosophies of the false teachers by saying, "These are wells without water"; literally, "springs without water." Of what value is a dried-up spring to a thirsty traveler? Likewise, of what value is Spiritless teaching to thirsty souls? The Lord Jesus said in John 4:14, "Whosoever drinketh of the water that I shall give him shall never thirst; but the water that I shall give him shall be in him a well of water springing up into everlasting life." Those who drink of the Water of Life, Christ Jesus, shall never thirst again. It is our privilege to drink constantly at the fountainhead with the assurance that every spiritual need will be met. God promises in Matthew 5:6, "Blessed are they which do hunger and thirst after righteousness: for they shall be filled." Isn't it wonderful to know that, if one is thirsty for the Living Water, he may go to the Lord and drink freely and fully. God assures us in Psalm 145:18, "The Lord is nigh unto all them that call upon Him, to all that call upon Him in truth." Have you drunk of the Living Water, Christ Jesus? Are you saved and do you have the assurance of salvation? If not, come to Him and drink; for only He can satisfy the innermost longings of your heart.

A Yale University student was driving down to New York City with his date from Smith College for an evening of jazz and a good time. On the way it occurred to him that it might add to the frivolity of the evening to take in the much-publicized Billy Graham, who was having his big New York Crusade at Madison Square Garden. The student had heard Billy once before, earlier that year, when Billy spoke at his fraternity house.

"However," said the boy, "Billy grated me with his audacity in saying that we regular-living guys were sinners." So the cocky student thought this would be a good opportunity to go back and really have a laugh at Billy's expense.

Later in recounting the experience he said, "I didn't laugh much that night in the Garden. Sitting there among eighteen thousand people, I felt strangely alone. I sensed emptiness in my heart that anthropology, sociology, physics, art, jazz, women, and drinks had not been able to fill. Gradually I saw that Christ was the answer and that

He desired to fill the aching void in my heart. I struggled as I thought, what would my date think if I gave myself to Christ? How foolish I would look standing up and walking down in front of all those people. In that moment of crisis I suddenly realized that Christ loved me and there was no reason for me to resist His love. From the second balcony I wended my way forward, and that night Christ filled my heart. He has never failed me since."

Shortly after he made his decision for Christ, this young fellow started a Bible study group in his dorm at Yale. Later he enrolled as a student at Fuller Theological Seminary in Pasadena, California, to prepare for the ministry.

How do we explain such a mighty transformation? The answer is very simple: when one believes on Christ, he finds living, satisfying water, the Water of Life. The false teachers of whom Peter speaks knew nothing of the reality of this satisfying water. They were trying to lead others to contentment and peace, but they were merely blind leaders of the blind. The satisfaction they were offering to thirsty souls was that which the devil still offers to restless and distraught humanity—fleeting satisfaction through pleasure, lust, and uncleanness.

Perhaps you may recall this incident, which was reported in our newspapers several years ago. The Pope received the ninth wife of playboy Tommy Manville, Anita Manville, and bestowed upon her a blessing. Not only this, he also conveyed a blessing for Tommy as well. Mrs. Manville revealed to reporters afterward that she had told the Pope plainly, " 'But we are sinners.' He replied that sinners were to be pitied, but he gave his blessing to us just the same." Said Mrs. Manville, "I sent a wire to Tommy right away saying, 'You had better be a good boy from now on, because you have just been blessed.'"

What a pity that someone did not open the New Testament and tell this self-confessed sinner how to get victory over sin by receiving Christ as Saviour and Lord. Trying to be a "good boy" because the Pope had blessed him left poor Tommy right where he had been for a long time, and wife number nine as well. Is not such a religion that overlooks the seriousness of sin as empty as the false teaching of Peter's day? Surely it merits the same description—"wells without water."

But before leaving this graphic statement of Peter's, let us consider something else of importance. Very often water, as used in Scripture, refers to the Holy Spirit. For example in John 7:37-39 we read, "In the last day, that great day of the feast, Jesus stood and cried, saying, If any man thirst, let him come unto Me, and drink. He that believeth on Me, as the scripture hath said, out of his belly shall flow rivers of living water. (But this spake He of the Spirit, which they that believe on Him should receive: for the Holy Ghost was not yet given; because that Jesus was not yet glorified.)" The "rivers of living water" flowing forth from the Spirit-filled believer could also be translated, "springs of living water." In a very definite sense, every true believer in Christ should be as a spring of water, bubbling forth with the refreshing Water of Life for thirsty souls who need Christ. Such usefulness for the Lord can only be known as one is fully committed to the control and direction of the Holy Spirit. Souls are not won to Christ through human genius, intellect, or energy, but through the power of the Spirit of God at work in a consecrated life. This is made clear in Zechariah 4:6, where God says, "Not by might, nor by power, but my My spirit, saith the Lord of hosts."

There are few of us who do not realize the necessity of the Spirit-filled life for specific acts of service and ministry. But do we realize the extreme need of living in the Spirit at all times, even while engaged in the ordinary and so-called secular details of life? A trifling disobedience, a tiny sin, a microscopic indulgence may be enough to render the whole life powerless. It is for this reason that God implores us in Ephesians 5:18, "Be filled with the Spirit." This really means that we are to "keep on continually being filled with the Spirit." We must drink daily of the Spirit's fullness if we are to be as springs of water, overflowing with the Living Water.

Charles Haddon Spurgeon has said, regarding the importance of Spirit-filled living: "If we do not have the Spirit of God it is better to shut the churches, to nail up the doors, to put a black cross on them and say, 'God have mercy on us.' If you ministers have not the Spirit of God you had better not preach and you people had better stay at home. I think I speak not too strongly when I say that a church in the land without the Spirit of God is rather a curse than a blessing. If you have not the Spirit of God, Christian worker, remember that you stand in somebody else's way. You are as a tree, bearing no fruit, standing where a fruitful tree might grow." These are words of wisdom which every child of God would do well to consider.

How can the believer tell whether he is a bubbling spring of water, Spirit-filled, giving forth the Water of

Life? The test is very simple. He will have a deep concern for the souls of men. He will be living, not for himself, but for others, seeking to reach them for Christ. In his first Epistle Peter wrote, "Sanctify the Lord God in your hearts: and be ready always to give an answer to every man that asketh you a reason of the hope that is in you with meekness and fear" (1 Peter 3:15). The Spirit-filled believer will be ready always to give a word of witness for Christ. He will look for opportunities to lead others to salvation through the Saviour. If one's experience with the Lord is shallow and immature, he will have little concern and interest in being a witness for his Saviour.

A fourteen-year-old girl drowned in a motel swimming pool at Monterey, California. Several persons sat casually looking on without even attempting to help. Said the local fire chief who was summoned to the scene, "Why someone didn't dive into the relatively shallow water and get the girl out before it was too late I'll never know." The chief pulled her out of the pool, but it was too late.

It is difficult for us to imagine people sitting and watching a girl drown before their eyes. But is this not an example in miniature of why millions are hastening on to eternal death today? So many who say they are Christians live placidly on the sidelines, engaged in selfish interests, rather than make an attempt to rescue the lost and point them to Christ. These Christians need above all else the filling of the Holy Spirit that from their innermost being may flow forth springs of Living Water; that those on every hand who are dying from spiritual thirst might find Christ.

Peter tells us also that the false teachers were not only

"wells without water" but "clouds that are carried with a tempest; to whom the mist of darkness is reserved for ever." They were as mist or fog, driven by a tempestuous wind. Here Peter presents the picture of a violent storm, breaking forth from black thunderclouds with destructive gusts of wind and floods of rain, resulting in catastrophe. Is this not descriptive of what false teaching does for empty hearts? Rather than provide peace, it results in turmoil and confusion. False teaching cannot possibly quiet the storms of life. Only Christ can.

Do you remember the incident recorded in Mark 4? Jesus had been teaching from early morning until late afternoon. He invited His disciples to come with Him to a small boat. Shortly after they departed for the other side of the sea, weary from the long day of teaching, our Lord fell asleep in the hinder part of the ship. Not far along the course of their voyage the sky darkened, the winds blew, and the waves tossed the little craft to and fro. Soon the storm unleashed its fury. Slowly the ship filled with water. Finally in desperation the disciples awakened Christ crying, "Master, carest thou not that we perish?" Did He not care? Why, certainly! He always cares for His own. What did He do? We read in Mark 4:39 that "He arose, and rebuked the wind, and said unto the sea, Peace, be still. And the wind ceased, and there was a great calm."

As the Lord Jesus calmed the storm in that hour of need, He provides peace and serenity for every storm of life even now. False teaching cannot do this; unbelief cannot do it; but our Lord can. He says to every troubled heart: "Peace I leave with you, My peace I give unto you: not as the world giveth, give I unto you. Let not your heart be troubled, neither let it be afraid" (John 14:27). Are you restless, disturbed, distraught, tossed about amidst the confusion and perplexities of life? Then turn to the Lord Jesus Christ and find peace and calm.

Peter further reminds us of another of the fallacies of the false teachers. Though they appeared to be very clever and intelligent, yet it was definitely a case of "talk without walk." "For when they speak great swelling words of vanity, they allure through the lusts of the flesh, through much wantonness." They were like those described by Paul in Titus 1:16, "They profess that they know God; but in works they deny Him, being abominable, and disobedient, and unto every good work reprobate."

As we consider this evil of the false teachers, it might be well for those of us who are Christians to ask ourselves the question, "Do we *walk* on Monday and the rest of the week as we *talk* on Sunday?" It is essential that we walk the same at all times. As children of God we are to follow the Lord, "He that saith he abideth in Him ought himself also so to walk, even as He walked" (1 John 2:6).

THE LIVING SERMON

I'd rather see a sermon than hear one any day,
I'd rather one would walk with me than merely tell the way,
The eye's a better pupil and more willing than the ear;
Fine counsel is confusing, but example's always clear.
The best of all the preachers are the men who live their creeds
For to see good put in action is what everybody needs.

I soon can learn to do it if you'll let me see it done,
I can watch your hands in action but your tongue too fast may run;
The lectures you deliver may be very wise and true,
But I'd rather get my lessons by observing what you do.

I may not understand the high advice that you may give
But there's no misunderstanding how you act and how you live!
—Author Unknown

A blind man was found sitting at the corner of a street on a dark night in a great city with a lantern beside him. Seeing he was blind, a man went up to him and asked why he had the lantern, for light to a blind man would be the same as darkness. The blind man replied, "I have it so no one will stumble over me."

Think of that for a moment! He bore a light so no one would stumble over him. Do our friends and neighbors stumble over us because we are failing to let our light shine for Christ? Where one man reads the Bible, a hundred read you and me. Paul wrote to the Corinthians, "Ye are our epistle written in our hearts, known and read of all men" (2 Corinthians 3:2). Though many around us have no time or regard for the Bible, they do watch Christians and "read" their lives.

The world may have its arguments for unbelief, but no argument can stand against a convincing life of holiness and obedience. An atheist once said, "I can stand all the arguing of Christian apologists, but I have a little servant who is a disciple of Jesus Christ and her pure, honest, truthful life staggers me sometimes."

The one irresistible argument for the gospel and its power is a regenerated and consecrated life. It is for this reason we are told in Colossians 3:1-3, "If ye then be risen with Christ, seek those things which are above, where Christ sitteth on the right hand of God. Set your affection on things above, not on things on the earth. For ye are dead, and your life is hid with Christ in God." Let your life count for the Lord. Do more than talk Christ; live Christ! The false teachers of Peter's day spoke with fluency, but their wicked lives voided every word they uttered.

You will notice, too, that the false teachers directed their godless theories at those who were babes in the faith. This is the procedure the adherents of false doctrine usually follow. Peter speaks of "those that were clean escaped from them who live in error." I am prone to believe that "those that were clean escaped" were true children of God, but probably babes in Christ. The false teachers were seeking to entice them away from the truth. In spite of this satanic thrust through the false teachers, these immature believers "clean escaped," they overcame and continued on for the Lord. It is so important that all of us who know Christ grow in the Lord. Only then can we withstand the evil attacks of the enemy.

The false teachers promised liberty, but Peter informs us that they knew nothing of liberty in themselves for "while they promise them liberty, they themselves are the servants of corruption." They were still mastered by their sinful hearts. As long as a man is controlled by sin, he is the servant of sin. Thus Peter says, "For of whom a man is overcome, of the same is he brought in bondage." The false teachers were bound by the shackles of lust and wickedness. Because of their persistence to continue in sin and because they refused to submit to the deliverance Christ provides, they were captives, binding themselves tighter and tighter in the chains of iniquity. They could have experienced deliverance, but they chose to remain "the servants of corruption," prisoners to their own evil works.

During one of the early French wars a man who was called Louis the Strong made bows for French archers. These were of such fine workmanship that no one man ever broke a bow made by Louis the Strong. One day the French took a number of prisoners and the governor of the prison sent for Louis.

"I want you to make me some strong chains," he said, "for the garrison prison will hold no more men. So I must keep my prisoners in the courtyard. Therefore, the chains must be very strong or they will break them and escape." Louis had never made chains but he replied, "I think I can do what you want, for I have some very fine metal which I will temper so no man can break it." He was as good as his word. He made chains such as had never been made. By degrees the authorities of the prison discarded all the old chains and used only those made so cunningly by Louis the Strong.

In the course of time Louis committed a treasonable act and was declared guilty. He was put in prison and manacled. Sitting in his prison cell he examined the chains by which he was bound. Suddenly he was heard to cry out, "Horror of horrors, these are my own chains! Had I but known I was forging them for myself, how differently I would have made them!" The chains that bound him were such as no living man could break, and they were worn by the hands that made them. Helpless and hopeless, Louis sat bound, a prisoner in a dungeon, held by chains of his own forging.

There is a sense in which the same was true of the false teachers of whom Peter speaks. "For of whom a man is overcome, of the same is he brought in bondage." By their refusal to heed the truth, by their open rebellion to submit to the Lordship of Christ, by giving allegiance to the devil, they hardened their own hearts and chose their own paths, leading to ultimate judgment and perdition. But is it not true that all men outside of Christ, by their continual neglect of the Saviour and their persistence in following the paths of sin, are forging a chain which they can never break? Link by link, by their bad habits and their sins, they are making a chain which shall hold their souls in endless captivity.

Is there no escape? Yes, there is, at this moment, by yielding to Christ. False teaching cannot deliver, but Christ can. Have you entered into the liberty that God has provided for all who come to the Saviour? The Lord Jesus said, "And ye shall know the truth, and the truth shall make you free. . . . If the Son therefore shall make you free, ye shall be free indeed" (John 8:32,36).

Some years ago Henry Drummond was traveling to an appointment by carriage and team. Along the way he fell into conversation with his carriage driver. The great preacher was astonished to learn that his driver had once been a prominent professional man, but because of a vicious personal habit which he had been unable to master, he had fallen deeper and deeper into sin and finally was compelled to seek employment as an unskilled laborer. During the conversation the driver earnestly appealed to Mr. Drummond for help. After reciting some accepted rules for breaking the power of bad habits, the celebrated preacher asked the driver this question: "Friend, if your team were running away with you, even after you had used every means within your power to hold them, what would you do if you suddenly learned there was a person sitting beside you who knew exactly how to control your team and save you from disaster?"

"Sir," the driver replied quickly, "I would hand over the reins to him." Then Mr. Drummond told him about Jesus Christ who is able to control our life if we but hand over the reins to Him.

Christ can control unholy tempers, undisciplined angers, unruly tongues, and unrighteous lives. But we must hand over the reins to Him. Do you know the victory of a Christ-controlled life? You may be a child of God, but have you submitted to the Lordship of Christ? Is He your Master today? If He is, there is no habit He cannot break and no temptation He cannot overcome. Submit to His control fully! He says, "My grace is sufficient for thee: for My strength is made perfect in weakness" (2 Corinthians 12:9). Are you weak, defeated, discouraged? Bow to your Saviour and Lord, claim His perfect strength by surrendering to His rulership and control.

Should it be that you have not yet come to Christ for salvation, remember, you are like the false teachers of whom Peter speaks, in that you are a servant of corruption. You will never know deliverance from the power of sin until you come to know Him who gives victory over sin. His blood cleanses from all sin. Will you claim Christ as the Lord of your life at this moment?

13.

RETROGRESSION

"For if after they have escaped the pollutions of the world through the knowledge of the Lord and Saviour Jesus Christ, they are again entangled therein, and overcome, the latter end is worse with them than the beginning."—2 Peter 2:20

In Luke 9:62 we read the words of our Lord Jesus Christ who said, "No man, having put his hand to the plough, and looking back, is fit for the kingdom of God." Our Lord makes it clear that it is extremely dangerous to make a profession of faith only to retrogress later and to turn back to the former ways of life. It is this evil that Peter warns against as he tells us of the false teachers who had a knowledge of Christ and salvation, but who reverted to the old paths of unbelief and sin. The consequences of retrogression are lamentable: "for if . . . they are entangled therein, and overcome, the latter end is worse with them than the beginning."

It would seem from the initial reading of the words of our text that those of whom Peter writes had been saved;

"they have escaped the pollutions of the world through the knowledge of the Lord and Saviour Jesus Christ." Though this may seem to confirm that they were Christians, note carefully the fact that they had only a "*knowledge* of the Lord and Saviour Jesus Christ." Knowledge about Christ and the way of salvation is not enough to save.

To be sure, one cannot be saved without knowledge. Romans 10:17 makes it clear that "faith cometh by hearing, and hearing by the word of God." Knowledge is attained through the Word. In fact, the Word of God is the only dependable and true source of knowledge for salvation. When religious cults add a "manual" or "key" as a supplement to the Bible, it is always safe to say that "the Scripture and something 'plus' is *unscriptural*." Knowledge of Christ and of the way of salvation obtained from the Word is the means to faith and belief.

The false teachers of which Peter writes "escaped the pollutions of the world" in the sense that they stood on the verge of deliverance. Had they responded to the knowledge which God gave them from the Word, they would have been saved. Rather than receive Christ into their lives, they professed salvation and merely pretended to be Christians. Later they rejected the truth altogether and turned back into sin.

Someone may ask, "Is it not possible for one to be saved and to go back into sin?" Certainly it is. What believer in Christ has not experienced this regrettable calamity at some time? One thing is certain, however: if a man or a woman is truly born of the Spirit, even though he may fall back into sin, he will not stay in sin. Peter tells us that the false teachers were "again entangled therein, and overcome."

Sin was their master, controlling their lives. There was no evidence of God's grace working in their hearts.

The Lord not only saves the one who comes to Christ, and transforms his life; He sustains and gives victory over sin. In 1 Samuel 2:9 we are assured that "He will keep the feet of His saints." In Psalm 23:6 God's servant declared, "Surely goodness and mercy shall follow me all the days of my life: and I will dwell in the house of the Lord for ever." He did not say that he hoped to dwell in the house of the Lord some day; he was already assured of it. He was certain that God would enable him to be loyal and faithful. "Surely," was as much as to say " *I am sure* goodness and mercy shall follow me all the days of my life." In Philippians 1:6 we read, "Being confident of this very thing, that He which hath begun a good work in you will perform it until the day of Jesus Christ." Further we see in 1 Thessalonians 5:24 that God declares, "Faithful is He that calleth you, who also will do it." The Lord will not fail those who love Him. He will faithfully uphold us for, as Jude declared, "He is able to keep you from falling, and to present you faultless before the presence of His glory with exceeding joy" (Jude 24).

Someone put this startling question to an elderly saint of God who was lying on her deathbed.

"Now, Nannie, what if after all your praying and waiting God should suffer your soul to be lost?" The dear woman raised herself on her elbow, turned to him with a wistful look, laid her hand on her Bible, and then replied, "Is that all the faith you have?" Her eyes sparkled with heavenly brightness as she said, "God would have the greatest loss. Poor Nannie would but lose her soul and that would be a great loss indeed; but God would lose His honor and character. Haven't I hung my soul upon His exceeding great and precious promises? If He breaks His Word, He would make Himself a liar and the universe would rush into confusion." These wonderful words of truth were among the last that fell from the lips of this child of God.

Praise God, the true believer in Christ can sing:

> Blessed assurance, Jesus is mine!
> Oh, what a foretaste of glory divine!
> Heir of salvation, purchase of God,
> Born of His Spirit, washed in His blood.

Do you have this blessed assurance? Could it be that you are like those of whom Peter wrote, who had a knowledge of Christ, but who did not possess Christ? It is possible to have a full mind but an empty heart. An empty heart is a greater misfortune than an empty purse. Is there no hope for an empty heart? Ah, yes, for the Bible says "That if thou shalt confess with thy mouth the Lord Jesus, and shalt believe in thine heart that God hath raised Him from the dead, thou shalt be saved. For with the heart man believeth unto righteousness; and with the mouth confession is made unto salvation" (Romans 10:9-10). Here is good news for every troubled heart. This is God's message of hope for every distraught and distressed soul. Believe in your heart that God raised Christ from the dead. Believe in your heart that what Christ did He did for you. By believing, you will receive deliverance from sin as well as the power to live and walk in the Christian way of life. Though your heart may be stained with sin, God says in Isaiah 1:18: "Come now, and let us reason together, saith the Lord: though your sins be as scarlet, they shall be as white as snow; though they be red like crimson, they shall be as wool." God desires to transform your life, giving you victory over sin.

An immense block of Carrara marble stood in a cathedral courtyard in Florence, Italy. An inexperienced sculptor had blocked it out carelessly and ruined it for the statue he had planned. Too costly to destroy, too tremendous to move, and thought too imperfect for use, it lay unused for nearly one hundred years.

Then, in 1501, Michelangelo, the famous young Italian artist, was chosen to fashion and perfect the statue, which was to have been called "The Giant." Carefully he measured the block of marble, taking special note of the injuries, concluding that he would have to make a tall thin figure. As he thought of Bible heroes, he suddenly knew that he wanted to portray David, the young shepherd lad who was a giant, not in stature but in faith.

Quickly he began to sketch, planning to utilize every possible inch of the huge marble block. He had a shed built over the stone, and soon the sound of his chisel could be heard morning, noon, and night. . . . After three years of almost continuous labor Michelangelo's David was completed, towering eighteen feet high, and weighing nine tons, magnificent in every line, one of the great master's greatest works. One of Michelangelo's own students on seeing it cried in wonder, "Master, it lacks only one thing, and that is speech." A masterpiece of art was created from a rejected block of marble.

Wonderful though that work of genius may seem, it is nothing in comparison with what God does with a sinful heart when a man or woman fully trusts in Christ for redemption. The Lord changes the life completely. You may be sure, if one is genuinely transformed by the power of God, there will not be a permanent retrogression to sin. On the other hand, the victorious believer will keep going forward in the way of blessing, growing in grace, desiring to please and obey his wonderful Lord.

Occasionally we hear people ask, "How do I know that what you are teaching about salvation as taught in the Bible is true? Are there not other ways of salvation being taught from the same Bible?" It is true, there are various plans of salvation being offered. In fact, a pastor commented about it to his congregation, after hearing religious broadcast after broadcast on the previous Sunday, while in another city.

"Not once," he said, "did I hear the plain truth of salvation." Indeed there must be multitudes of people who listen to religious broadcasts on the Lord's day who must be greatly confused at the clamor of voices concerning religious matters. Each claims to have the truth, yet many are in seeming conflict with one another. How can one know who is right? Or we might even ask, is there any "right" belief at all?

I am convinced that there is a way that is "right," that can stand all the tests. Not only can this way be found, but the finder can surely know that he has discovered the truth. Let me give a few basic principles whereby one ascertains this.

First, understand thoroughly that you are not seeking a mere system or belief: you are looking for truth. Secondly, use the Bible for your authority. This is God's inspired Word. What man has to say is of little value unless it can be traced to the Scriptures. Do not accept anyone's word for it but go to the Bible yourself, carefully search it, and read it with a desire to know the truth. Thirdly, be sure that God will reveal truth to any earnest and seeking heart. He longs to reveal His Word to those who want to know it. So be sure God is on your side, if you are a seeker after truth. Fourthly, as you read and study the Bible, recognize it as God's Word. Believe what it says and accept it and heed it as though God were speaking to you. Fifthly, shun any individuals or groups that place more weight on books that explain the Bible than on the Bible itself. If you are really sincere and before God you are honest in your desire to know the truth, I believe that if you follow these few simple rules it will not be long before you will be a possessor of the truth rather than a searcher for truth. God says in Luke 11:9, "Ask, and it shall be given you; seek, and ye shall find; knock, and it shall be opened unto you."

After one comes to the knowledge of the truth, what is the next step? Believe the truth! As one believes on Christ, he receives the Son of God as his Saviour and Lord. The tragedy of the false teachers, of whom Peter speaks, was this: after searching for the truth and finding it, they did not sincerely believe it. As the result, they were worse off than they had been before they knew the truth.

To know the truth and to do nothing about it is probably the most sorrowful and regrettable experience anyone can have in this life. Consider what God says in Hebrews 10:26-29: "For if we sin wilfully after that we have received the knowledge of the truth, there remaineth no more sacrifice for sins, But a certain fearful looking for of judgment and fiery indignation, which shall devour the adversaries. He that despised Moses' law died without mercy under two or three witnesses: Of how much sorer punishment, suppose ye, shall he be thought worthy, who hath trodden under foot the Son of God, and hath counted the blood of the covenant, wherewith he was sanctified, an unholy thing, and hath done despite unto the Spirit of grace?" How can one read these verses and proceed to reject or neglect Christ? God makes it clear that if one receives a knowledge of the truth and then rejects it, there is no promise of hope. The final result is eternal judgment. To reject the gospel of Christ after knowing the way of salvation is to trample upon the blood of Christ with hatred and disrepute. Never has there been and never will there be a more serious offense in the universe.

It is for this reason that I plead with you to consider at this very moment the claims of God on your soul. Have you ever stopped to consider God's great love for you? His concern for your salvation sent His beloved Son to the cross. Even though you have sinned thousands of times against Him, His love for you has never changed. He says in Jeremiah 31:3, "I have loved thee with an everlasting love: therefore with lovingkindness have I drawn thee." With outstretched arms of compassion God is reaching for you today, seeking to draw you to Himself. He wants you to be saved through His Son that you might know the "peace of God, which passeth all understanding" (Philippians 4:7).

I am told that the cost of the last war was $2,200 a second, $132,000 a minute, $7,920,000 an hour. The citizen who paid an income tax of $1,000 a year paid for less than a half-second of war. There is no way of measuring the cost per second of the war of the soul on God. Everyone outside of Christ is at war with God. Actually he is warring against light, life, peace, joy, and satisfaction, which are all to be had freely in Christ Jesus. In Acts 23:9 the Bible says, "Let us not fight against God." Many are fighting against God today. As long as this warfare is on, it is impossible to have peace. War extinguishes peace. Throw down your arms of rebellion against the Lord who loves you. Say to Him, "I surrender unconditionally to Thee, my Lord, my God." Then you will know the blessed experience of Romans 5:1, "Therefore being justified by faith, we have peace with God through our Lord Jesus Christ."

Do you have peace? If you are outside of Christ, you do not, because you are a sinner; and in the sight of God you are a wicked sinner. The Bible declares in Isaiah 57:20-21: "But the wicked are like the troubled sea, when it cannot rest, whose waters cast up mire and dirt. There is no peace, saith my God, to the wicked." "No peace!" Those who have not believed in Christ are totally devoid of even the slightest concept of the peace of God. In Romans 3:17 Paul declares, "The way of peace have they not known." But to his own blood-bought children our Lord says, "Peace I leave with you, My peace I give unto you: not as the world giveth, give I unto you. Let not your heart be troubled, neither let it be afraid" (John 14:27).

Let us be reminded that there is no one too far gone for the Lord Jesus Christ to save. One may be a hardened sinner, filled with lust and wickedness. His appears to be an impossible situation, but it is not impossible for God. Doubtless you have read in Luke 8 about the wild man of Gadara. No one could do anything with him. He was a constant menace and threat to the community. The people had given him up as a hopeless case. When the Lord Jesus met him, He healed him immediately. The people of the city heard the news. They could not believe it. So they came out to see for themselves and they found the wild man "sitting at the feet of Jesus, clothed, and in his right mind" (Luke 8:35).

Christ knows your need better than you do yourself, for He created you. He understands your circumstances perfectly. He will handle all your problems if you will but place yourself in His care and really give Him a chance to prove Himself (Malachi 3:10; Hebrews 3:9). But you must believe Him. You must receive Him as Saviour and Lord.

Peter makes it clear that the latter end of these who reject Christ is worse than the beginning. The beginning is bad enough because man without the Lord lives in the energy of the flesh. God has created all men to enjoy Him. When He made man, God left a place in the human heart which was intended for Himself. Most people seem to have only an empty void where God ought to be. Such a beginning in life is most disastrous. But the end is even worse, by far. The culmination of such a life is to be eternally separated from the God of love and grace. It is to be cast into endless perdition, never again to know anything that is good, wholesome, or right.

Many give no thought whatsoever to their future. To them, the subject of final retribution for sin is ridiculous.

They are planning for this life only. Like the Epicureans of old, they live for today. Their philosophy is very simple: "Eat, drink, and be merry, for tomorrow we die." They are far more concerned about eating and drinking than about dying. But God assures us that death is inevitable; and after death there is nothing but endless misery for those outside the Saviour.

A brilliant young man recently graduated from a large college here in the United States. On graduation day he was seen walking across the campus with one of the professors.

"Jim, what do you plan to do upon graduation?" asked the professor.

"Oh," said Jim, "I plan to go to law school and hope to become a successful lawyer."

"After that what?"

"No doubt I will gradually get into politics, for I have a yen for public life," replied Jim.

"That is interesting," said the professor, "but then what?"

"Who knows, I might even become governor of our state," was Jim's reply.

"Excellent," parried the professor, "and what after that?"

"By then," said Jim, "I will be getting on in years. I believe I will have enough money and with my family all grown, my wife and I can travel, for I have always wanted to see the world."

"Sounds wonderful," said the elder, "but what then, Jim?" Jim thought a minute, then with braggadocio said, "I suppose there is nothing left but call it a day and die."

"And what after that, Jim?" the voice of experience persisted. There was a dead silence; no plans had been made beyond that.

Millions like Jim in our own land, even though they know about Christ and the message of the cross, have made no plans beyond death. God forbid that any of us will be foolish enough to plan day in and day out for a few short years on this earth and make no plans for an eternity to come. God says that a man who lives only for this life with no regard for the next is a fool.

Do you recall the Word of our Lord in regard to the rich unbelieving farmer of Luke 12? God had blessed the farmer abundantly, but rather than give the Lord the glory, the farmer "thought within himself, saying, What shall I do, because I have no room where to bestow my fruits? And he said, This will I do: I will pull down my barns, and build greater; and there will I bestow all my fruits and my goods. And I will say to my soul, Soul, thou hast much goods laid up for many years; take thine ease, eat, drink, and be merry. But God said unto him, Thou fool, this night thy soul shall be required of thee: then whose shall those things be, which thou hast provided?"

Are you wise in the eyes of men but a fool in the eyes of God? Repent before it is too late. Turn to Christ. God says in Luke 13:3, "Except ye repent, ye shall all likewise perish." Bow before the Lord. Acknowledge your sinfulness and claim His forgiveness. Christ shed His precious blood as a sacrifice for your sins. He did this for you that there might be a way of escape, an eternal escape from your sins, that you might be the possessor of eternal life. Do not be satisfied with knowledge about Christ; by faith receive Him into your heart and be assured of life eternal.

14.

REJECTION

"For it had been better for them not to have known the way of righteousness, than, after they have known it, to turn from the holy commandment delivered unto them. But it is happened unto them according to the true proverb, The dog is turned to his own vomit again; and the sow that was washed to her wallowing in the mire."—2 Peter 2:21-22

D. L. Moody used to tell of a mother he knew who had a child who was mentally deficient from birth. Naturally, this mother loved her baby in spite of his abnormality. As the child grew, it was necessary for the mother to give more and more of her time to care for her afflicted son. She gave up practically everything to devote herself to the hour-by-hour care essential to the child's well-being. After fourteen years of this kind of unselfish living, she was heard to say: "I have never considered anything I have done as a sacrifice. I have tended my child faithfully, and I love him with my whole heart. But there is one thing that disturbs me immensely, and it is this that is breaking my heart: my child does not even know me; to him I am no

156

different than anyone else; there is no response to my love."

What parent cannot understand this parable from life? Who of us does not sense the anxiety of this broken-hearted mother? A one-sided love can produce nothing more than grief and unhappiness. It was a matter of one-sided love as far as the false teachers of 2 Peter were concerned. With unending devotion the Lord showered His love upon these unbelievers within the church. He made the message of salvation clear and comprehensible to them, but there was no lasting response to His benevolence and grace. The same is true of many in our day. They have heard the way, they know the truth, but rather than receive the message of God they reject the Lord. What a sorrowful calamity, to be so near and yet so far. 

It is this that Peter warns against: "For it had been better for them not to have known the way of righteousness, than, after they have known it, to turn from the holy commandment delivered unto them." This is not to suggest that those who have never heard or known the truth will escape eternal judgment. The Scriptures are clear. Jesus declared in John 3:3, "Except a man be born again, he cannot see the kingdom of God." There is no question about it: unless one experiences the new birth by believing on the Lord Jesus Christ, ultimately he must be judged for his sins and cast into hell. Peter is making a comparison. He does not give the slightest indication that there is an escape for anyone who has not heard or known the truth. Eternal judgment must be meted out on all who fail to come to Christ, whether they know of Him or do not know of Him.

It seems, however, that there are degrees of punishment.

Doubtless those who have listened to the gospel repeatedly but have carelessly rejected the truth will suffer punishment of the worst degree. In all probability those who have never had an opportunity to hear will suffer a lesser punishment. This is not to minimize the horrors and anguish to be experienced in the throes of hell. Hell at best is the worst that could be experienced by anyone. What could be worse than eternal separation from God and His love? In addition to this, the sufferings of hell will be excruciating. Three times in chapter 9 of Mark's Gospel Jesus used the expression, "Where their worm dieth not, and the fire is not quenched" (Mark 9:44,46,48). If there were no other penalty, this would seem severe enough. But even more appalling is the fact that in hell there will never be another opportunity for anyone to receive Christ. Thus, we need to be reminded of the seriousness of the sin of rejection.

It may be that you are rejecting Christ without even realizing it. Some feel that to reject Him they must openly disalliege Him. One may say nothing or do nothing about receiving Christ. This is enough to reject Him. To neglect Christ is to reject Him. How many unsaved people there are, busily engaged in the mundane affairs of this life, who give no thought to the Saviour who loves them. Do not be guilty of the sin of rejection. Remember, after this life there is no second chance. God at this moment bids you to come and believe on His blessed Son that you might enjoy abundant life in this world and eternal life in the world to come.

It had been a stormy week in New York City. On one particular day the rain roared down on East 42d Street in a frightening fury, accompanied by the high sobbing of driving winds. The street was almost deserted, save for a lonely figure staggering along on his way to Grand Central Station. The cause of his staggering was not due alone to the anger of the elements, but also to the two large suitcases which he practically dragged. Every few minutes there was a sign that he would like to prop himself against a wall for a breather, but the rage of the rain and the wildness of the wind caused him to carry on. Only half a block now remained—but it appeared almost too much; he was ready to collapse. Suddenly, as out from nowhere, another figure appeared by his side. A cheery voice called out, and before he knew it the suitcases were taken from him in welcome but strange assistance.

"We're both going the same way," the stranger said in a booming voice that was somehow familiar, "I might as well help. You look as if you could use some." The traveler nodded in sheer relief. For the remainder of the journey he kept glancing at his unknown friend's face. There was something vaguely familiar about it, somewhere he had seen it . . . and the voice, too, something about it. . . . When they were within the safe shelter of the terminal he turned and asked the question which had preyed upon his mind.

"Please, Sir, what is your name? There is something about you. . . ." To his dying day, Booker T. Washington never forgot the thrill of the reply, "The name, my friend, is Roosevelt, Teddy Roosevelt"!

A famous hand of help in a time of need. How welcome! How appreciated! But what of that "more famous" help of the Lord Jesus Christ and Calvary for every sinner trapped by the storm of sin? Have you personally welcomed Him into your life? For your sake He willingly left the serenity of Heaven to dwell amidst the storms of this satanically-disrupted sphere. Our God is "ready to forgive; and plenteous in mercy unto all them that call" upon Him (Psalm 86:5). Thus I beseech you to "taste and see that the Lord is good" (Psalm 34:8).

Possibly someone will say: "I can understand why those who reject Christ must be judged and ultimately cast into hell. They had a chance to receive life, but they chose the consequences of rejection. But what about the poor souls who have never heard the gospel? Why should they be held accountable? Is it fair of God to thrust them into hell? They have never had a chance." If salvation were to be based on "fairness," would not all of us deserve hell immediately? Have we not "sinned, and come short of the glory of God" (Romans 3:23)? Not only are we sinful by nature but we are rebellious toward the goodness and mercy of God. We can thank the Lord that His judgment is not based on fairness, but rather on grace. David said in Psalm 145:8, "The Lord is gracious, and full of compassion; slow to anger, and of great mercy." Indeed, God is gracious. It is through His mercy that He forgives all our sins on the grounds of the sacrifice of His beloved Son, Jesus Christ.

We should not overlook the fact that up to the present, millions in our world today have never yet had an opportunity to hear the gospel. If they die in this state they are eternally lost. The Lord is not willing that they perish in their sins. He has fulfilled His responsibility by providing a way to be saved for all who believe. What about us? Are we doing our best to reach the lost for Christ? God not only saved us but commissioned us to go "into all the world, and preach the gospel to every creature" (Mark 16:15). Few of God's people are really serious about this responsibility. If convenient, they will go; after other things are cared for, they will go. But to accept this as the basic duty of Christian discipleship, they have failed, while millions of souls are hastening on to a Christless eternity.

In one of the relay races of the Olympic games the French team had started very well. The first two men kept up among the leaders, but as the baton was being passed to the third runner he dropped it. This put the team out of the running. The man who had dropped the baton threw himself upon the ground, held his head in his hands, and wept openly. His emotional outburst continued as he was led from the stadium. For a man to take defeat so tearfully might seem rather extreme were it not remembered how many people were involved in this member's failure. There were all the French Olympic athletes with their dashed hopes; there were the two runners who had put forth such effort and done so well, whose work had been ruined by one man's blunder; there was the runner who was to have come after the third runner, who never got to run at all.

Rarely does any man live unto himself. His failures usually affect many others. Never was this so true as it is of the Church of Jesus Christ which is failing miserably in its God-ordained responsibility to carry the gospel to every lost soul.

In the first chapter of the book of Acts the Lord Jesus

tells us that we are to be witnesses unto Him "unto the uttermost part of the earth." So often this verse is misquoted as "unto the uttermost *parts* of the earth." Jesus said "part," singular—"the uttermost *part* of the earth." This means if there remains but one spot on the face of the earth where the gospel has not gone, there would not be a complete fulfillment of the commission. In the Moroccan Arabic Bible "part" is translated very strikingly by a word meaning a "speck," such a tiny thing as you might get in your eye. Thus the Lord Jesus is actually saying that we are to bear witness unto Him "unto the uttermost *speck* of the earth." If there remains one "speck" upon this earth where Christ has not been proclaimed, it will not be one-hundred-per-cent fulfillment of Jesus' command.

The real problem we ought to be concerned about today is not what will happen to the heathen if they do not hear the gospel; the question that should disturb true disciples of Christ in this generation is what will happen to us if we fail to obey the great commandment of Christ to carry the gospel to everyone. In Ezekiel 3:18 God says: "When I say unto the wicked, Thou shalt surely die; and thou givest him not warning, nor speakest to warn the wicked from his wicked way, to save his life; the same wicked man shall die in his iniquity; but his blood will I require at thine hand." It is a serious offense to be guilty of the blood of another, yet who of us is not guilty today? Because we have lived for ourselves, because we have failed to sacrifice to do what God told us to do above all else, countless numbers of lost souls are still without the gospel.

What is the chief cause of our failure? The answer to this question is very simple: a lack of love for Jesus Christ. It is this fact that our Lord was endeavoring to convey to Simon Peter when He asked, "Simon, son of Jonas, lovest thou Me more than these?" (John 21:15) Until this occasion Peter had been wholly ineffectual as a witness for Christ. He was a believer, daily receiving showers of blessing from the hand of God; but he had not yet come to the joy of giving out for the Lord. What was the reason? His heart was fixed on earthly things rather than the heavenly. Many of our present-day believers are like Peter in this respect. After Christ did some probing in Peter's selfish heart, the apostle came to the place of unconditional and complete surrender to His Lord. He loved Christ with his whole heart, and almost immediately he became a missionary of the cross and went out to tell others of the Saviour and His great love. God will give you and me this same concern for the lost if we will but fall before Him, confessing a pure and unqualified love toward Him, at the same time bidding farewell to all that displeases Him.

Gustave Doré, the great French artist, had nearly completed one of his famous paintings of the face of Jesus. As he was in the act of putting on the delicate finishing touches, a lady stepped into his studio quietly and stood for a moment admiring the wonderful production of Doré's genius. Suddenly he became aware of her presence.

"Pardon, Madam, I did not know you were here," he said with his usual politeness. She smiled and said with touching earnestness, "Monsieur Doré, you must love Him very much to be able to paint Him so."

"Love Him, Madam?" he replied. "I think I do love

Him. But if I loved Him more I would paint Him better." Can it not be said of us that if we loved Christ more we would serve Him better? We would not live for ourselves. We would readily respond to the need of the hour to take the gospel to those who have never yet had a chance. No, let us not blame God for this failure; we have failed.

In the concluding verse of 2 Peter 2, the apostle by means of analogy informs us why the false teachers forsook the way of truth. Peter quotes from two old proverbs. One is found in the Old Testament, Proverbs 26:11: "As a dog returneth to his vomit, so a fool returneth to his folly." The other may have been taken from a source other than the Scriptures, since this is the only mention of a sow in the Bible. Both proverbs are not only true but vividly descriptive. As the dog returns to his vomit and the sow to its filth, so will one turn back to the old paths of sin if he has never been truly redeemed by Christ. Even though he may appear to be a believer for a time, as did the false teachers, sooner or later the truth will come out. The unsaved teachers, of whom Peter writes, appeared to be cleansed from their sins; but it was merely a surface experience. Theirs was a case of outward moral reformation but not inward spiritual regeneration. Like the dog returning to its vomit and the sow to its filth, so the false teachers reverted to the worst forms of sin, from which it had appeared they had been delivered. Without a genuine work of God in the heart it is impossible to be delivered from sin and lust. This cannot be achieved by moral reformation but only by divine regeneration.

D. L. Moody was twenty years old before he ever heard a sermon on regeneration. He was told to be good, but he later said: "You might as well tell a black man to be white as to tell him to be good without telling him how. You might tell a slave to be free, but that would not make him free. We are a bad lot, the whole of us, by nature. It is astonishing how the devil blinds us and makes us think we are so naturally good. Don't talk to me about people being naturally good and angelic; we are naturally bad, the whole of us. The first man born of a woman was a murderer. Sin leaped into the world full-grown, and the whole race has been bad all the way down. I have heard of reform until I am tired and sick of the whole thing. It is regeneration by the power of the Holy Ghost that we need."

Of course, if you talk to the average person about sin, he thinks you are old-fashioned or puritanical. His concept of a sinner is one who is behind iron bars in a penitentiary. Few realize their own sinfulness as seen by the eye of God. Be sure, He sees us as we are. David confessed in Psalm 69:5, "O God, Thou knowest my foolishness; and my sins are not hid from Thee." Further, the Lord tells us in Psalm 44:21 that "He knoweth the secrets of the heart." Little sins are as abominable in the sight of God as the big ones. In fact, it seems doubtful that God even distinguishes between little and big sins. In His sight all sin is abominable. What may appear to be insignificant or small to you or me may be of extreme magnitude in the judgment of God.

Do you know that one speck of dust in an automatic light control instrument is sufficient to cause a multimillion dollar supersonic jet airplane to veer widely off its course? Do you know that a tiny speck of lint from clothing or moisture from fingerprints can cause a guided missile, zooming along at twice the speed of sound, to go awry and miss its mark? Do you know that smog and humidity can cause intricate light instruments to fail and endanger the success of vital military missions? Small things are important. Especially is this true regarding sin. "A little leaven leaveneth the whole lump," God says in Galatians 5:9.

Let us suppose you have only one or two little sins in your life. What do you plan to do with them when you face a holy and righteous God? You will suddenly learn that you will be as guilty before God as the thief, the harlot, the drunkard, the murderer, and all other sinners. Doubtless you will plead, "God, I have not done the things these people have done." But God will say to you, "Have you read my Word?" And I believe He will quote Ezekiel 18:20, "The soul that sinneth, it shall die." These words can never be changed or altered. There will be no exceptions. Sin must be judged by death; all sin—big or little. There are no exceptions.

Oh, heed the message of truth before it is too late. Do not be like the false teachers who knew the way but rejected it. "The blood of Jesus Christ His Son cleanseth us from all sin" (1 John 1:7). God will forgive you at this moment and save you for eternity if only you will heed His voice and believe on His blessed Son. Consider Christ's words of invitation as found in John 10:9, "I am the door: by Me if any man enter in, he shall be saved, and shall go in and out, and find pasture." Come to Him and be saved. The door is open now. Soon it will be closed. This is your opportunity.

You may ask the question, as some have, "How can I be sure that God will save me?" The answer is: He told us so in His Word. God cannot lie. He never changes His mind. We need only accept His truth at face value. In John 5:24 we have the words of the Son of God Himself, "Verily, verily, I say unto you, He that heareth My word, and believeth on Him that sent Me, hath everlasting life, and shall not come into condemnation; but is passed from death unto life." Here you have it stated clearly and succinctly. When one truly believes on Christ he becomes a new creature in Christ and passes from death unto life. This may seem too easy; it is easy to a certain extent. It is easy for us but it was not easy for God; it cost Him the blood of His own beloved Son. "Christ died for our sins" (1 Corinthians 15:3).

Two men who had been friends in their youth met years later in the police court of a great city, one on the judge's bench, the other a prisoner. Evidence was heard and the prisoner found guilty. In consideration of their former friendship, the judge was asked to withhold sentence.

"No," he said, "that cannot be. Justice must be done and the law upheld." So he gave sentence: fifty dollars fine or fourteen days at hard labor. The condemned man had nothing wherewith to pay, so prison was before him. Then the judge, having fulfilled his duty, stepped down beside the prisoner, paid his fine, put his arm about him, saying, "Now, John, you are coming home with me to dinner." Thus the prisoner was set free because the judge paid the fine.

So it is with the great salvation God offers to all. He cannot overlook sin; He must be faithful and just, because of the righteousness of His holy nature; but He paid the price for sin. If you will receive Christ into your heart you will be forever delivered from the bondage and the penalty of sin.

15.

RETROSPECTION

"This second epistle, beloved, I now write unto you; in both which I stir up your pure minds by way of remembrance: That ye may be mindful of the words which were spoken before by the holy prophets, and of the commandment of us the apostles of the Lord and Saviour."—2 Peter 3:1-2

Peter begins the third chapter of his second Epistle by telling us why he wrote it: "This second epistle, beloved, I now write unto you; in both which I stir up your pure minds by way of remembrance." As in the first chapter, the apostle again emphasized the importance of looking back over the past—Retrospection. There are some things that should be forgotten; on the other hand, there are many things that must never be forgotten. Peter reminds us that we must never forget "the words which were spoken before by the holy prophets, and of the commandment of us the apostles of the Lord and Saviour." The Bible should be the believer's textbook, his rule of faith and practice. All he is and all he believes depends upon the credibility and veracity of this Book. But is it not dangerous to place such an emphasis upon a book? Not at all, when it is *the Book*, God's holy Word.

You will note that Peter speaks of stirring up our "pure minds." He is speaking to those who have believed on Christ. Apart from Christ there is no such thing as a "pure mind." Paul makes this clear in Titus 1:15, "Unto the pure all things are pure: but unto them that are defiled and unbelieving is nothing pure; but even their mind and conscience is defiled." When one believes on the Lord Jesus, the blood of Christ purifies not only the heart, but the mind. After the initial cleansing at conversion, there should be the continual cleansing of the heart and mind through the reading and study of the Word of God. Jesus said in John 15:3, "Now ye are clean through the word which I have spoken unto you." Believers who would have pure minds and pure hearts must be men and women who will spend time with the Lord, meditating on His Word. No one of us is equipped to begin the day until first of all he meets the Lord in His revealed Word. When a child of God opens the Bible, he has the inestimable privilege of entering immediately into the presence of the King of kings.

Alexander Maclaren realized this so thoroughly that before he read his Bible each morning, he would dress as neatly as he could, straighten his tie, comb his hair, and then sit down and open the Word. He made careful preparations to go before the King. Many people are more concerned about how they look to the eyes of others than they are about their appearance before God. Be that as it may, when the Bible is opened, we face the Lord of all, who speaks to us as we read.

No wonder, after finishing a season of meditation on the commandments of God, David cried out, "How sweet are Thy words unto my taste! yea, sweeter than honey to my mouth" (Psalm 119:103). He heard the voice of God speaking to his heart. This experience was not for David only; it is for you and me. But we must take time to permit God to speak to us from His Word. That is why Paul tells each of us in 2 Timothy 2:15 to "Study to show thyself approved unto God, a workman that needeth not to be ashamed, rightly dividing the word of truth." To study the Word of God does not mean the hasty reading of a chapter or two before rushing into the obligations of the day. Study requires time, concentration, searching, and the practical application of that which is studied. How few believers really study the Word.

Consider the time spent with newspapers, magazines, and television in contrast to the little time spent with the Bible. Recently an interesting survey was released by the American Management Association under the title, "How Much Time Should You Give to Reading?" The survey was conducted among business executives and brought forth some significant facts. The average company official spends two hours and forty-five minutes a day on "must" reading: reports, business correspondence, and related reading. An additional hour and a quarter is spent on "optional" reading, such as newspapers and books. The survey also found that he subscribes to an average of eight business magazines—all for the express purpose of increasing his value and efficiency and promoting his position with his company. His reading is important because it is imperative.

We might think further of the question, "How Much Time Should You Give to Reading?" and relate it to the believer's use of the Word of God. Mere mental recognition of the value of God's Word, however noble and proper, will not be sufficient to translate it into the important area of "must" reading. The Lord has always intended His Word to be a tool, as well as a treasure; an instrument, as well as an inspiration; a dynamic, as well as a delight. Our attitude toward this practical, down-to-earth phase of the Word as related to daily living directly determines the portion of time given to its study. It was F. B. Meyer who said, "We may measure our growth in grace in the measure in which we grow in the knowledge of the Word of God."

As the Israelites gathered manna in the morning, so we should feed on God's truths at the beginning of the day. Moses said to his people, "This is the bread which the Lord hath given you to eat. This is the thing which the Lord hath commanded, Gather of it every man according to his eating, an omer for every man, according to the number of your persons; take ye every man for them which are in his tents" (Exodus 16:15-16). The manna was given each morning. It had to be gathered early, before the heat of the day. It is in the Word that we find "the true bread from heaven" (John 6:32). We must get up early and gather a daily portion of it before the heat of the day and before the absorbing occupations of the day have invaded our hearts.

It was necessary, too, to eat all the manna gathered, otherwise worms would get into it. So Christ reveals Himself fully in the Word, but we can receive the benefit in proportion to that which faith appropriates. The children of Israel could not nourish themselves with the memory of what they ate the day before. We read in Exodus 16:21 that "They gathered it every morning, every man according to his eating: and when the sun waxed hot, it melted."

Beginning one's day with Bible study and prayer is like tuning up an instrument before beginning to play in an orchestra; like eating a meal before using the energy of body and brain; like absorbing sunshine and fresh air in vacation to help guard against illness during the cloudy, wet days of fall and winter. Those who make it a practice to take time every day, preferably at the outset, to read, meditate on, and pray over the Scriptures will testify with the Psalmist, "O how love I Thy law! it is my meditation all the day" (Psalm 119:97).

One important phase of Bible study that is frequently neglected by the people of God is that of Scripture memory work. Those who would get the most out of the Bible will do well to commit passages of the Word to memory. God's servant declared in Psalm 119:11, "Thy word have I hid in mine heart, that I might not sin against Thee." By hiding God's Word in his heart, I am quite sure he meant that he memorized the Word. As believers fill their hearts with the memorized Word, the Holy Spirit will unfold the truth, giving understanding and enlightenment. If the Word of God is not stored away in the heart, the Holy Spirit has nothing upon which to work.

Dr. James McConkey tells of a young man he used to meet at Bible conferences. The youthful believer was not an educated man, but he had set his mind on getting a knowledge of the Word of God by memorizing a verse a day. Dr. McConkey tells that when he first met this eager Bible student, he had been working on this plan for eight years. During that time, he had committed over two thousand verses of Scripture to memory. When he prayed it was like a rich brocade of silver and gold of the Word of God, interwoven with praise, testimony, and petition. It was a thrilling thing to hear that young man, a workman in a steel mill, give his testimony for God. What this sincere and earnest believer did, we can do.

Frequently I hear people say, "I just can't memorize anything." It is not a case of *can't* memorize, but *won't* memorize. Memorization of the Word of God is not easy. The devil hates God's Word, and he will do everything to discourage the believer from memorizing it. The mind is naturally lazy and needs to be whipped into action. But if we would best enjoy the precious truths God has given to us in His Word, we must take time to memorize Scripture.

The day may come, and soon, when we shall regret the fact that we did not memorize more of God's Word. In many parts of the communist world the Bible has been taken from God's people. All they have of the Scriptures is that which they took the time to store away in their hearts years before. How grateful they are that they have this to which they can cling. Recently I heard of a "Bible Eating Society." This is an organization of young Christians who are studying the Word in an all-out attempt to memorize as much of it as possible in the light of present communist persecution. They are committing scores of Scripture passages to memory; in the event that the time comes when they have no Bibles, they can still draw on the Word from their overflowing hearts.

Peter desires that we "be mindful of the words which were spoken before by the holy prophets, and of the commandment of us the apostles of the Lord and Saviour." Are you being mindful of the Word of God? Are you purifying your mind by the use of the Word? Do you honor and respect the Bible as God's truth?

Recently, a little boy in New Jersey risked lateness at school to wait for a letter which his father, before his death, had arranged that the son should receive on his birthday. On each birthday until he becomes of age, and then on his wedding day, the son is to receive a letter which the father entrusted to some unknown friend. When asked about the contents of the first letter, the mother of the boy said it was too sacred to be made public. I am sure all of us can appreciate the interest and concern that must have been in the heart of that young lad as he read the letter from his deceased father. Doubtless he is looking forward to reading each remaining letter with the same concern.

Child of God, you and I have a letter from our Father above. He is not dead but eternally alive. In this letter He has written that which you and I need most to face the problems and confusion of life. If we are to enjoy it, we must take the time to read it. Do you think the little boy read his deceased father's letter and then tore it up and threw it away? I am sure he must have read it and reread it time and time again. The child of God who is in love with his Father through Christ will do the same.

In his last interview with George Müller a friend asked the aged saint of God, "Excuse me, but how many times have you read the Bible through?"

"Well," replied George Müller, "as you ask me, I may say that I have read it through sixty-six times, and I am now going through it for the sixty-seventh time and it gets sweeter and more interesting every time I read it." Is this your testimony, too? Can you say as David of old, "The law of thy mouth is better unto me than thousands of gold and silver" (Psalm 119:72)? Is God's Word really precious to you?

We hear much in these days about the need of revival. I firmly believe that one of the important requisites for revival is a return to the Word of God. As the Word is faithfully studied, believed, practiced, and preached, doubtless revival will be the result.

A little girl went to Sunday school and church with her girl friend. Later in the day, her mother asked what the sermon was about. The preacher had preached on revival. The little girl could not pronounce her "v's," so she said "rebible." Is it not true that if we are to see revival there must indeed be "rebible," a return to God's Word?

There is a crying need in our day that the Bible be brought back to a place of prominence in our pulpits. The aged Paul gave young Timothy a charge, which is recorded in 2 Timothy 4:1-4: "I charge thee therefore before God, and the Lord Jesus Christ, who shall judge the quick and the dead at His appearing and His kingdom; Preach the word; be instant in season, out of season; reprove, rebuke, exhort with all longsuffering and doctrine. For the time will come when they will not endure sound doctrine; but after their own lusts shall they heap to themselves teachers, having itching ears; And they shall turn away their ears from the truth, and shall be turned unto fables."

The apostasy described in these verses has been witnessed clearly in the age in which we live. Many preachers have become too intelligent for the Bible. They are preaching a "gospel of opinion" rather than the facts of God's inspired Word. From this gospel of opinion flow rivers of poisonous serum, paralyzing the church and rendering it impotent. The proclamation of the gospel of opinion has led to all manner of weird, extreme excesses, evil pursuits, and warping eccentricity. It has led to rationalism, modernism, mysticism, subjectivism, and spiritualism. The hosts of cults, sects, and false religions are its prize creation.

To describe this deadly disease a little more in detail we would indicate that it is "egoism" in the extreme. The "I" with its opinions, convictions, and intuitions is the seat and center of all authority. Instead of the Word of God, one's "humble opinion" is the basis of truth. In many churches the congregation is being opinionized to death rather than being evangelized to life. It is the devil's wily device, for it is destruction. In the final analysis, the reason for the vigorous preaching of the gospel of opinion is that people are determined to endorse and justify the way they live at any cost. It is a convenient way to make God the author of their sins. Anyone or anything can be justified or condemned within the elastic limits of the gospel of opinion.

On one occasion the Apostle Paul declared, "Woe is unto me, if I preach not the gospel!" (1 Corinthians 9:16). Indeed we may say woe unto any man who professes to be called of God and yet neglects to proclaim the unsearchable riches of the Word of God. How many there are in our pulpits today who at one time knew the truth, but they have allowed the crafty and shallow doctrines of men to supplant the knowledge of God's Word.

A Christian friend tells of talking recently with a young minister who, over the past few years, has fallen for the delusion of a liberal ministry. This liberal clergyman made the statement, "I am living in hell." Only a few years ago he was a promising, young, regular army officer. Called of God into the ministry, he resigned his commission and gave up a military career. He had been advised by sincere believers to be careful in selecting his seminary. Listening to the counsel of others, however, and feeling secure in his convictions, he enrolled in a well-known denominational seminary. The first year he strongly resisted liberalism; the second year he decided to keep quiet; the third year he began to be unsure and doubts arose, especially concerning the reliability of the Scriptures. He had learned to doubt and question everything but he had been given none of the answers. No wonder he is "living in hell" today. How can he possibly help others?

Equally disturbing is the fact that there are many, who profess to be true followers of the Lord Jesus, sitting and listening to these false teachers who are proclaiming the deceitful lies of the devil. Is it not as sinful to listen to a liberal week after week and to support his diabolical ministry with God's money as it is to be a liberal?

I have met sincere believers in Christ all over our country who are still holding membership in modernistic churches where they are not being fed from the Word of God. At the same time, though they do not realize it, they are growing cold in their own hearts. Why do they stay in such an environment? The usual answer is they feel that God needs them there to give out the Word of God. I often ask these individuals, "How many souls have you led to

Christ in that atmosphere during the past year?" Few have any to report. Granted there are some in those churches really trying to do a work for God; but the real reason many of them stay is that they do not want to be labeled as a fanatic. They want to be well spoken of by everyone. Are we to be men-pleasers or God-pleasers? Are we to care for ourselves or are we to proclaim the gospel of truth? Those who take a sincere stand for Jesus Christ will often suffer persecution; they will be laughed at and ridiculed. God has not promised an easy way for believers. They persecuted our Lord and finally put Him to death. The same may happen to us if we stand true to our Saviour.

A small group of Christians were led to break away from a worldly church. They formed another and were greatly blessed of God. But they were much spoken against by those in the other church, whose minister on meeting a newly converted man said to him in a haughty manner, "I hear you have been converted since you left us to join the new sect."

"That's right, Sir," was the courteous reply, "but I don't know what you mean by 'sect.' I was a member of your church for many years and I never knew I had to be converted. But in this 'sect' as you call it, I found Christ as my Saviour and Lord, and I am truly a thankful man."

Often Christians will be criticized and ridiculed for being faithful to the Lord. But what is more important in life than knowing Christ and taking a consistent stand for Him? Of what value are all the thousands of dollars being poured into a local church if that church is not teaching the Word of God to the children, young people, and adults that come? Unless the Bible is preached and taught, these are all wasted dollars that will be as fruitless as Christless preaching and teaching.

It has been said that most people who join churches in our day join by "confusion of faith" rather than "confession of faith." They have heard so little of the Word and know even less about it. Consequently, they are rushed into a church simply to help in the process of building a "big church" which is powerless and useless. God has declared that "The Word of God is quick, and powerful, and sharper than any twoedged sword, piercing even to the dividing asunder of soul and spirit, and of the joints and marrow, and is a discerner of the thoughts and intents of the heart" (Hebrews 4:12). He further says in 2 Timothy 2:9, "The word of God is not bound." He has given us a Book which contains His message for us in the "words which were spoken before by the holy prophets." This Book is not only to be honored and respected; it is to be believed and practiced. Irrespective of what people say against it, it will continue to stand long after its critics have been buried and disintegrated into dust, for God declares in Isaiah 40:8: "The grass withereth, the flower fadeth: but the word of our God shall stand for ever."

Child of God, what are you doing with the Word of God? Are you using it as God intended? Are you permitting Him to speak to you daily from His blessed Word? He desires to stir up our "pure minds by way of remembrance." But if we are not men and women of the Book, there is very little He can do in and through us. Let us thank God that we have the Bible. There are many saints throughout the world who want it but do not have it.

A fifteen-year-old Korean boy longed to possess a Bible

all his own. But his parents were poor; they could not afford to pay his school tuition, let alone buy him a Bible. In church one Sunday his pastor announced that the Bible Society men would come to the village with copies of the Scriptures to sell. He added that the Bible Society would accept whatever farm produce the village folks should offer in exchange for the Scriptures. They would accept even rice-straw ropes, brooms, and other such items. When the boy heard that announcement, he felt that his opportunity had come. He would make straw rope. He thought he was the happiest boy in the world; he could not stop smiling. As soon as he returned home he began to make rice-straw rope. He started early in the morning and worked late into the night. By the time the Bible truck came to the village, he had made 455 feet of rope. As soon as the truck stopped in front of the village church, he ran to it, carrying the bundle of rope in both arms. He handed it to the man in charge, who gave him a beautiful New Testament. When his hands held the copy, two lines of tears were flowing down his cheeks, but his face was bright and smiling.

Possibly the Lord made it too easy for most of us to have a Bible. Maybe if we had to make rope or perform some other laborious task to get a copy of the Scriptures, we would appreciate the Word of God more. If the Bible has not had the place in your life that God intends that it have, confess your shortcomings to Him at this moment. Pray with David, "Open Thou mine eyes, that I may behold wondrous things out of Thy law" (Psalm 119:18). Vow before the Lord to spend time in the blessed Book so that He can speak to your heart daily.

Let me offer just one further thought. Should it be that you have never definitely received Christ into your life, be mindful of the fact that until you know Him, God's Word will be meaningless. Make certain that you have believed on the Lord Jesus Christ; then the Word of God will be illumined by the Holy Spirit and the message of God will be clear and simple. Let Christ have His perfect way in your heart and life as you receive Him as Saviour and Lord.

16.

REFUTATION

"Knowing this first, that there shall come in the last days scoffers, walking after their own lusts, And saying, Where is the promise of His coming? for since the fathers fell asleep, all things continue as they were from the beginning of the creation."—2 Peter 3:3-4

One of the recognizable characteristics of the "last days," Peter tells us, will be the appearance of "scoffers" who will seek to refute the claims of God's holy Word. "There shall come in the last days scoffers, walking after their own lusts, And saying, Where is the promise of His coming?" Were the scoffers to remain outside the church, hurling their venomed shafts at the Scriptures, denying the truths of God's infallible Word, the problem would not be so serious. But in our day, it is within the church that the spirit of denial is rife. The scoffers have infested the church of Jesus Christ as never before. They have "crept in unawares," as Jude reminds us, seeking by their subtle teaching to turn away the hearts of believers from the truth. The Word of God is being discredited and its authority and inspiration derided. For a true believer to say that he believes the Bible to be the very Word of God without admixture of error is to make him an object of severe ridicule. In many churches the preachers either by-pass the Holy Scripture or spend a portion of their time making apologies and excuses for it. To them Jesus is mere man, perhaps more cultured and refined than others with a greater mastery of Himself, but nevertheless a man.

Thus, the fundamentals of our faith are being called in question today, not from the outside, but from within: in our pulpits, in our seminaries, and as the result, in many so-called Christian homes. But as Peter says in verse 2, we must "be mindful of the words which were spoken before by the holy prophets," for God declares, "The law of the Lord is perfect, converting the soul: the testimony of the Lord is sure, making wise the simple" (Psalm 19:7).

The severest attack the scoffers make on Christian truth is discovered in their derision of the doctrine of the Second Coming of Jesus Christ. In Peter's day the scoffers argued, "Where is the promise of His coming? for since the fathers fell asleep, all things continue as they were from the beginning of the creation." The scoffers have not changed much. Many in our contemporary pulpits seek to explain away this basic truth of the Word of God. Many more say nothing about it. The great majority of their regular listeners on Sunday morning are totally ignorant of even the scriptural statements regarding the return of Christ.

While pastoring a church in St. Louis, Missouri, I was approached at the conclusion of one of the Sunday morning services by a visitor who expressed her appreciation for the sermon she had just heard on the Second Coming of Christ. Upon inquiry I learned that she was from Kansas City, Missouri, where she was a member of a large and flourishing church.

"In fact," she said, "I have been a member and a regular attendant at that church for twenty-five years. Rarely have I ever missed a service, and as far back as I can remember, I have never heard one sermon on the Second Coming of Jesus Christ." What a tragedy that sincere, interested people have been left in the dark relative to this important fact of Scripture.

If the truth of the return of Christ were barely mentioned in the Bible, one could understand why some would neglect to emphasize its importance. But looking into the Word of God, what do we find? The Old Testament abounds in prophecies, giving special emphasis to the Second Coming of Christ. By far the greatest number of prophecies concerning Christ in the Old Testament tell of His Second Coming. Of the forty-six Old Testament prophets, less than ten speak of the First Coming of Christ, while thirty-six speak of His Second Coming. In the New Testament there are over three hundred verses emphasizing Christ's return. One out of every twenty-five verses refers directly to our Lord's Second Coming. The only subject mentioned in the New Testament more than the Second Coming is that of faith.

It is impossible to study the words of Christ without noticing that our Lord refers to His return at least twenty-one times. Of the twenty-seven books in the New Testament, all but four of them refer to it. Fifty times or more in the New Testament we are exhorted to be ready for the realization of this blessed hope. Paul mentions baptism just fifteen times but he mentions the Second Coming fifty-five times. In his Epistles, with the exception of Galatians and Philemon, the Second Coming is mentioned many times. Entire chapters, such as Matthew 24 and 25, Luke 21, and Mark 13, are devoted to the subject, as are whole books such as 1 and 2 Thessalonians and the Revelation. Thus, anyone who professes to be a believer in Jesus Christ and does not proclaim the truth of the Second Coming of Christ either does not know the Word of God or he is seeking intentionally to silence it.

What are some of the reasons why the scoffers reject the truth of the return of Christ? The liberal theologian despises it because the return of Christ would prove the liberal to be a liar. All his rationalistic theories would be exposed as falsehood. When our Lord comes again, those who have claimed that the Bible is not the Word of God but merely *contains* the Word of God will be faced immediately with the fact that the Bible is indeed the inspired Word of God, inerrant and unfailing. Christ's return will prove that all that the Bible says about Jesus concerning His virgin birth, His sinless character, His divine power, and His bodily resurrection from the dead actually transpired as recorded in the Bible. The return of Christ will mean a death blow for liberalism. Some day the liberal will have a rude awakening when he discovers that all that God has said in His Word is absolutely true.

Another reason why some scoff at the doctrine of the return of Christ is that they associate this great truth with many of the radical cults of our day. These scoffers are usually nominal Christians. They shy away from anything that might have any tinge of fanaticism. This scoffer knows little about the Bible because he does not read the Bible. He is untaught and untrained regarding God's truth. Consequently he forms his own opinion about anything he may hear from the Word of God. Thus, by his ignorance he denies one of the most important themes of scriptural truths.

Then there is the intellectual scoffer who is fearful that he may be classified as an ignoramus if he were to stoop to such a "fantastic" thing as belief in the return of Christ. This scoffer likes to appear to be intelligent and scholarly and fears being looked upon with disrepute by his acquaintances, were he to embrace such a repugnant theme as the return of Christ.

There is also another scoffer who teaches that the kingdom of God will be brought in by the efforts of humans. He is busily engaged in the propagation of a false program whereby the church will convert the world. He is blind to all that is transpiring around him, for he boldly asserts that the world is getting better and better all the time. He expects that soon it will reach the golden age. He scoffs at the teaching of the Second Coming for it is contrary to his viewpoint. The Scriptures teach that this age in which we are now living will end with seven years of great tribulation. During this time morals will be at their lowest, character will be at its worst, and respect for others will be unknown. The scoffer who believes in a better world strongly castigates the teaching of the Second Coming because he is not a man of the Word of God; he is a follower of tradition.

Probably the most common scoffer of all is the man who

wants to live for himself. He has set up his own pattern and plan and has no time to think about the return of Christ. He has set up his idols and is not concerned about waiting for God's dear Son. He refuses to search the Scriptures to seek God's teaching on the matter. He prefers to live on undisturbed, enjoying his own selfish exploits.

The chief scoffer of all is the devil himself. He seeks to repudiate the claims of God as they are advanced in the Scriptures relative to the glorious appearing of Christ. He blinds the minds of those that would believe. He tempts men and women to choose man's theories in opposition to God-revealed truth. Satan hates the thought of the return of Christ because he knows that it will mean doom for him.

Scoffers—there are many of them in our day. You need not go far to find them. "Where is the promise of His coming?" they ask, "for since the fathers fell asleep, all things continue as they were from the beginning of the creation." Consider the thousands of years that have gone by. Christ has not returned yet. Is this not proof enough that the teaching of the return of Christ is ridiculous? Such an argument seems plausible. But regardless of what men say, God says, "I will shake all nations, and the desire of all nations shall come" (Haggai 2:7). "And the Lord shall be king over all the earth: in that day shall there be one Lord, and His name one" (Zechariah 14:9). "And He shall judge among many people, and rebuke strong nations afar off, and they shall beat their swords into plowshares, and their spears into pruninghooks: nation shall not lift up a sword against nation, neither shall they learn war any more" (Micah 4:3). "For the earth shall be filled with the knowledge of the glory of the Lord, as the waters cover the sea" (Habakkuk 2:14).

To every born-again believer God declares, "Be ye also patient; stablish your hearts: for the coming of the Lord draweth nigh" (James 5:8). Christ will return! The word of God assures us that it is so! Where is the promise of His coming? God's Word is the promise. Believe it, receive it, watch for the King of kings to return. "Therefore be ye also ready: for in such an hour as ye think not the Son of man cometh" (Matthew 24:44). We are not told when Christ will return. This is not our business. We are not on the time committee; we are on the preparations committee. We are to watch and wait, keeping busy for God, anticipating His return.

Scores of books have been written on the Second Coming by false cults, many of them declaring that He has already come. Such writings are ridiculous. His coming will not be viewed by a few but by everyone. The Word of God is clear: "Behold, He cometh with clouds; and every eye shall see Him, and they also which pierced Him: and all kindreds of the earth shall wail because of Him" (Revelation 1:7). The entire world will know about the return of Christ. Let us not be concerned about the time; rather let us be certain that we know Him, having submitted to His Lordship, so that we are ready to meet Him when He comes. What a day of rejoicing and glory that will be for the child of God who has communed with his Lord and walked with Him down through the years. In the hours of testing the believer has voiced his petitions to God with the assurance that his wonderful Christ will not fail him. Indeed He has not failed. But oh, the joy of knowing that some day—at the time of His glorious return—we shall see Him as He is!

A beautiful story is told of a young Englishman, a member of a family of wealth and high social position, who had been blinded by an accident when he was but a lad of ten. In spite of his physical handicap, this young man won high university honors as an exceptionally brilliant scholar. Also he had won the hand of a beautiful bride, the daughter of a high-ranking officer in the British navy. A short time before their marriage was to have taken place, this young man, William Montague Dyke, had submitted to a course of treatments and a surgical operation, which had been performed by a famous specialist. Although he loved his fiancée dearly, the young bridegroom-to-be had never looked upon her face.

The climax came on the wedding day as the guests, many of whom were representative of royalty, began to assemble. Among those attending were cabinet ministers, generals, admirals, bishops, and distinguished men and women of letters. Sir William Hart Dyke stood arm-in-arm with his son, the bridegroom, for the eyes of the young man were still swathed in bandages. Standing near by was the famous eye specialist who had met them in the vestry of the cathedral. The beautiful bride entered on the arm of her father and drew near the waiting group. Not a word was spoken for the moment was so tense that all were beyond speech. Was her lover actually to see her face, which he had known only by the touch of his delicate finger tips? The great surgeon cut away the last bandage. The bridegroom stepped forward with that hesitant uncertainty which is characteristic of those who have known long years of blindness. A shaft of rose-colored light shone through the stained glass of the cathedral windows and illuminated his face, but he did not see it, for his wondering gaze was fixed upon the face of her who was to be his bride. She had loved him dearly even when he was blind. For long minutes they gazed into each other's faces and finally from his lips came these awe-filled words, "At last! . . . at last!"

This true story of an actual happening is one of tremendous dramatic power. But it is merely a hint, a faint suggestion of a scene which will take place some day in the light of eternity's shores, when the child of God will look upon the face of the Lord Jesus. God says, "For now we see through a glass, darkly; but then face to face: now I know in part; but then shall I know even as also I am known" (1 Corinthians 13:12). As pilgrims we are journeying through a world pervaded with trial and sorrow. But as our footsteps falter, we are cheered by the blessed hope that some day we shall see Him who is the lover of our souls. After the bandages of human blindness have been cut away, then shall we know as we are known. This will be the climax of God's great love story for His own. Soon we shall gather for the marriage supper of the Lamb. "Behold, the bridegroom cometh," (Matthew 25:6). Are you watching for Him? Most important of all, are you ready to meet Him? Do you know the Lord? Are you saved? Christ is coming back again. Receive Him into your heart immediately if you never have.

We often hear human nature referred to as a stream— *the stream of humanity*. As the stream has its source in the high lands, the virgin snow-clad peaks, so human nature had its beginning with God. As a climax to everything else, God made man in His own image for fellowship with Himself. But as the stream leaves its source, so man turned from God, leaving Him out of his life, and lived as though God did not matter. The stream flows downhill, seeking irresistibly the lowest levels. Human nature, too, seeks its lowest level—down, down, down—to moral decay and spiritual ruin.

As the stream moves along, it is constantly picking up dirt and carrying it along, adding to its corruption. But here and there in its path are rocks that will not move with the stream. These will not yield to the irresistible descent; these rocks help to purify the stream. There are rocks in human nature, people who refuse to budge—Christian folks, solid, clean, and courageous. They will not yield to the descent.

Finally the stream finds its way to the ocean and pours itself into it. Human nature, too, ends in an abyss unless it allows itself to be lifted by the Son of God who laid down His life on the cross to redeem it. When a person yields to the pull of the Son, he is lifted back into fellowship with God. Are you in fellowship with Him? Do you know Him? Is He the Lord of your life? If not, bow in humble repentance before Him at this moment, for the Coming of the Lord draweth nigh. You need to be ready to meet Christ when He comes. Unless you have received Him as your Saviour and Lord, you are not ready. Believe on Him, then go to His Word, get hold of His message, study the Scriptures, see what the Lord has to say about the return of His beloved Son. Don't be a scoffer, as many are. Take God at His Word. Accept His truth wholeheartedly. Recognize the Second Coming as one of the pinnacle truths of Scripture upon which the Church of Christ stands.

Some years ago, Dr. Louis T. Talbot was giving a series of addresses on the theme, "The Return of the Lord Jesus to the Earth." One night a pastor of another church in the same town slipped in to see what Dr. Talbot might say about the Second Coming. No sooner had Dr. Talbot pronounced the benediction than this gentleman walked down the aisle and said, "I cannot agree with you on this subject."

"Well, I gave you God's Word. Your controversy is with Him, not with me," replied Dr. Talbot. The two preachers talked until the late hours of the night.

The next day one of Dr. Talbot's congregation, who had overheard a part of the conversation, telephoned him and said, "I do wish you would not get into these arguments." She ended by saying, "After all, you know that the subject is not a vital one. Suppose Christ should come or suppose He should not come, what does it matter anyway?"

All day long this thought bothered Dr. Talbot— "Suppose He should not come." He went to the Word to see what was dependent upon the return of the Lord Jesus and to see what takes place when He comes. Among the many things he found, this impressed him most: if Christ should not return, not one grave in this world containing the body of a child of God would ever open. Every Christian would have died in vain as far as the resurrection of his body is concerned. Your mother, your child, your husband, your wife, will remain as dust in the grave if Christ does not come. There is not one promise in the Word of God of the resurrection of the body that is not related to the return of Jesus Christ to the earth. "For the Lord Himself shall descend from heaven . . . and the dead in Christ shall rise first" (1 Thessalonians 4:16).

The dead in Christ are in every part of the habitable globe. They are in graveyards; they are beneath the waves of the sea. It has been estimated that there are more than three million of God's people buried in the catacombs of Rome. God declares that the dead in Christ shall rise first and they will meet the Lord in the air. When will that resurrection take place? When the Lord comes. If you take the return of Christ away from the Bible, you lock and bar every cemetery; trampling down the clods of dirt, you must write across the tombstone, "Never More to Live."

The Lord Jesus says in John 14:19, "Because I live, ye shall live also." When shall we live? We read in 1 Corinthians 15:22-23: "For as in Adam all die, even so in Christ shall all be made alive. But every man in his own order: Christ the firstfuits; afterward they that are Christ's at His coming." There is no question about it. When Christ comes, the graves of God's dear people will be opened and they shall meet Him face to face. What a blessed hope! What a comforting and assuring hope! Is this hope your hope? Do you know Christ as Saviour and Lord?

Maybe you have religion but not Christ. Come to the Saviour! You need not understand all about the Bible. Some of us have been studying God's Word for years. There are many things that we cannot completely comprehend. Much will never be fully known until we meet

Christ face to face. But God has revealed enough so that anyone who wants to may know how to be saved. The Lord Jesus says in Matthew 18:3, "Verily I say unto you, Except ye be converted, and become as little children, ye shall not enter into the kingdom of heaven." If you are willing to humble yourself in God's sight as a little child humbles himself before his parents, honoring and respecting them, you can be saved. Will you at this moment believe on Christ? He died and rose again that you might have life. He is a wonderful Saviour. Trust Him and see!

17.

REFLECTION

"For this they willingly are ignorant of, that by the word of God the heavens were of old, and the earth standing out of the water and in the water: Whereby the world that then was, being overflowed with water, perished: But the heavens and the earth, which are now, by the same word are kept in store, reserved unto fire against the day of judgment and perdition of ungodly men."—2 Peter 3:5-7

The false teachers sought to refute the doctrine of the return of Christ on the grounds that "all things continue as they were from the beginning of creation." Immediately Peter grasps the opportunity to reflect upon the past, thus revealing the profound ignorance of the false teachers. He begins by saying, "They willingly are ignorant." The word "ignorant" used here means "blind to the facts." What a hopeless state they were in. How could they possibly have any understanding of the truth? Theirs was willing ignorance; they did not want to know the truth. They were like the ostrich who buries his head in the sand to avoid the facts. As is the case of all unregenerate men, they lacked spiritual perception. "The natural man receiveth not the things of the Spirit of God: for they are foolishness unto him: neither can he know them, because they are spiritually discerned" (1 Corinthians 2:14). Except there is a divine quickening by the Spirit of God as the result of faith in Christ, the truth cannot be understood.

The real problem of these false teachers was that of unbelief. Not only were they ignorant of spiritual truth, but theirs was a voluntary ignorance. Though they knew the facts, they refused to accept them. Probably this is one of the worst of all sins. Unbelief is the closed door that shuts out the unsaved from the love, mercy, and peace of God.

Bertrand Russell, the famous British philosopher, gave the world the now infamous "ten commandments" of liberalism. The first of the ten reads, "Do not feel absolutely certain of anything." How pitifully weak unbelief is. Without a sure footing, without an anchor for the soul, with no "thus saith the Lord," man is as a cork on the waves, as a wandering star in an unknown universe.

In contrast, how wonderfully blessed is the Christian who is established on the absolutes and certainties of God. The true believer, unlike the unbeliever, has received the facts. The first is the fact of the Supreme Being: "In the beginning God" (Genesis 1:1); the second, the fact of Jesus Christ: "Jesus Christ the same yesterday, and to-day, and for ever" (Hebrews 13:8); the third, the fact of the inspiration of the Bible: "Thy word is true from the beginning" (Psalm 119:160); the fourth fact, the incarnation of Christ: "The Word was made flesh" (John 1:14); the fifth fact: the atonement of Christ, "Christ died for our sins" (1 Corinthians 15:3); the sixth fact, the assuring promise that all who receive the Lord Jesus Christ are the children of God: "But as many as received Him, to them gave He power to become the sons of God, even to them that believe on His name" (John 1:12). There are scores of other facts revealed in God's eternal Word; but these, if believed, will open the heart to the glories of eternity, providing the child of God with an everlasting song of joy.

Christ came into the world on the wings of song. All who know Him are able to sing. Unbelief has no music, no anthems, no hymns, no oratorios, no symphonies. When Robert Ingersoll, the noted agnostic, died, the printed notice of his funeral said, "There will be no singing."

Several years ago, H. L. Mencken, the agnostic editor of the American Mercury, died an unbeliever. At his funeral, following his request, there was neither song nor sermon. During his life, Mencken admitted he might be wrong in his views about God and the immortality of the soul.

"But," he explained, "if I am wrong I will square myself when confronted in the afterlife by the apostles with the simple apology, 'Gentlemen, I was wrong.'"

Mencken knows better now. He has found out that it was not as simple as that. After death it is eternally too late to repent or "square oneself" if wrong. Five minutes after death every infidel, every agnostic, every unsaved person will want to repent and seek an escape out of the place of torment in which he will find himself. But it will be too late. Now is the time to repent and turn to God. Ignorance and unbelief will provide no excuse in hell. The

Scriptures are clear, "Be not deceived; God is not mocked: for whatsoever a man soweth, that shall he also reap. For he that soweth to his flesh shall of the flesh reap corruption; but he that soweth to the Spirit shall of the Spirit reap life everlasting" (Galatians 6:7-8).

In answer to the argument of the false teachers that "all things continue as they were from the beginning of creation," Peter reflects on an important incident of the past which they had willingly overlooked. He reminds them of the flood, which was a definite divine interruption and intervention in the normal processes of the course of life: "that by the word of God the heavens were of old, and the earth standing out of the water and in the water: Whereby the world that then was, being overflowed with water, perished."

Peter points out several things here. One is that the heavens and the earth were created "by the word of God." With the current teaching of evolution, we should not skip hurriedly over this statement of Scripture. Some think the theory of evolution is comparatively new, but it is to be found in the philosophies that were being taught long before the birth of Christ. Wherever you find that which is true or genuine, you always discover a counterfeit close at hand. It was not long after Genesis 1:1 was recorded in God's Word—"In the beginning God created the heaven and the earth"—that Satan went to work forming a philosophy that might turn the minds of unbelieving men and women away from this truth. But nothing more sublime is found in all the realms of literature than the first ten words of Genesis. The world and the universe in which we live is not a conglomeration of chance elements.

Looking to nature we discover not chaos, but cosmos; not aimless chance, but definite evidence of design and order.

Dr. Alfred Russell Wallace, in *Man's Place in the Universe,* speaks of a host of marvelous adjustments in the world about us. He calculates that if the earth's density were only one-tenth less than it is, almost the whole of it would be reduced to snow and ice-clad waste. If the earth were larger than at present, the results would be even more drastic. If the earth were different, whether smaller or larger, life as we know it could not exist. All this points to a supreme, all-wise Creator of whom Peter declares, "By the word of God the heavens were of old, and the earth standing out of the water and in the water." The earth we inhabit and the universe of which we are a part is the result of God's creative fiat, His divine handiwork.

Sir Isaac Newton had a friend who, like himself, was a great scientist. The friend was an infidel while Newton was a devout believer. They often locked horns over the question of "Who made it?" though their mutual interest in science drew them together frequently. Newton had a skillful mechanic make him a replica of our solar system in miniature. In the center was a large guided ball representing the sun, and revolving around this were smaller balls fixed on the ends of arms of varying lengths, representing Mercury, Venus, Earth, Mars, Jupiter, Saturn, Uranus, and Neptune, in their proper order. These balls were so geared together by cogs and belts as to move in perfect harmony by turning a crank.

One day as Newton sat reading in his study, with this mechanism on a large table near him, his infidel friend stepped in. He was a scientist, who could recognize at a glance what was before him. Walking up to it he slowly turned the crank and with undisguised admiration watched the heavenly bodies move in their relative speeds in their orbits. Standing off a few feet he exclaimed, "My, what an exquisite thing this is. Who made it?" Without looking up from his books, Newton answered, "Nobody." Quickly turning to Newton the infidel said, "Evidently you did not understand my question. I asked who made this thing?" Looking up now, Newton solemnly assured him that nobody made it but that the aggregation of matter had just "happened" to assume the form it was in. But the astonished infidel replied with some heat, "You must think I am a fool. Of course somebody made it and he is a genius and I would like to know who he is."

Laying his book aside, Newton arose and laid a hand on his friend's shoulder.

"This thing is but a puny imitation of a much grander system whose laws you know," he said. "I am not able to convince you that this mere toy is without a designer and maker. Yet you profess to believe that the great original from which the design is taken has come into being without either designer or maker. Now tell me, by what sort of reasoning do you reach such incongruous conclusions?" The infidel was at once convinced and became a firm believer.

Let us not be deceived by the satanic and diabolical teachings of the day. Professors and false teachers "set themselves . . . against the Lord, and against His anointed, saying, Let us break their bands asunder, and cast away their cords from us" (Psalm 2:2-3). Doubtless God is sitting in the heavens laughing at poor, deluded men in their futile attempt to explain away the truth of creation as found in the Scriptures (Psalm 2:4). But let us never forget, irrespective of what unbelieving men teach: God's Word remains true.

Further, in reflecting on the past, Peter assured the false teachers that, since God created the heavens and the earth by His Word, He possessed the power to destroy His creation. "Whereby the world that then was, being overflowed with water, perished." This does not mean that the world itself was destroyed but that all life existing at that time perished as the result of God's judgment.

Thus the false teachers were in error. All things did not "continue as they were from the beginning of the creation." We may be sure also that in the future they will not continue as they were from the beginning of creation. Peter reminds us of the great conflagration that God will send upon the earth in the future at which time the earth will be purged by fire.

The only reason that life continues to exist and the earth, the sun, the moon, and the stars maintain their prescribed order in the universe at the present, is—as Peter tells us—that "the heavens and the earth, which are now, by the same word are kept in store." The same God who created the heavens and the earth by his Word "keeps in store" or sustains the universe by His mighty power.

Judgment will never again be meted upon the earth in the form of water, but Peter tells us that there will be judgment by fire. This will climax "the day of judgment and perdition of ungodly men," the Great White Throne judgment. This will be a sorrowful affair. The wicked of every age will stand before a holy, just, and righteous God to be judged for their sins. Nothing is more certain than this judgment. This momentous day was set long ago in the counsels of the omnipotent God. The pages of Sacred Writ reveal the fact that we are drawing near to that day when the books will be opened and the true characters of men will be revealed—judgment.

The purpose of the Great White Throne judgment will not be to decide whether one is guilty or innocent. God already knows this. It will be to manifest, to classify, and to assign the guilty sinner to the destiny for which he has prepared himself and to which he belongs.

The basis of the judgment will not be on the grounds of one's morality or his religion, but his attitude toward Jesus Christ. The Bible says in John 3:18, "He that believeth on Him is not condemned: but he that believeth not is condemned already."

No lost sinner will escape this judgment. The wicked dead will be raised to join the living dead. All will be there. Though man has been free to rebel against God, he will not be free to escape the consequences. The Lord Jesus made this fact so clear in John 12:48: "He that rejecteth Me, and receiveth not My words, hath one that judgeth him: the word that I have spoken, the same shall judge him in the last day." We are living in a day of grace at the moment. It will not always be so. Those who reject God's grace must ultimately face God in judgment.

It is interesting to note that when our Lord began His public ministry on earth, He gave a series of pronouncements, which we call the Beatitudes because each one begins with the word "blessed" (Matthew 5:3-12). He closed His public ministry with a series of pronouncements well entitled the "woes," since each of them begins with the word "woe" (Matthew 23:13-33).

We read in John 1:17, "For the law was given by Moses, but grace and truth came by Jesus Christ." What happened? Did this grace which Christ brought into the world fail? He began by telling of grace but ended speaking of judgment. Assuredly grace did not fail. Our Lord was teaching that when men spurn and reject grace and truth, they must certainly come to judgment. A careful reading of the Beatitudes will reveal that they were spoken to the disciples; but the woes were pronounced against those who not only refused to become disciples of the Lord Jesus, but sought to hinder others from following Him. For those who refuse to come to the Lord, judgment is certain. God says to the unbeliever, "Thinkest thou . . . that thou shalt escape the judgment of God?" (Romans 2:3) Many seem to feel that because God is so loving and kind at present He will excuse them in the future.

An irreligious man in one of the western states, who gloried in his unbelief, wrote a letter to the local newspaper in these words: "Sir, I have been trying an experiment with a field of mine. I plowed it on Sunday; I planted it on Sunday; I cultivated it on Sunday; I reaped it on Sunday; I carted the crop to the barn on Sunday; and now, Mr. Editor, what is the result? This October I have more bushels to the acre from that field than any of my neighbors have." He expected a commendable reply from the editor, who was not a particularly religious man himself. In the paper the next week there was the farmer's letter printed just as he had sent it. But underneath it was the short but significant sentence: "God does not always settle His accounts in October."

As certainly as judgment came upon the world by means of the flood, another judgment is coming. Doubtless before the flood, in spite of the fact that God had warned the people, most of them were indifferent and uninterested. Probably they said, like the false teachers of Peter's day, "all things continue as they were from the beginning of the creation." Why get excited? Why be disturbed? The flood came in spite of their reasonings. So judgment will come upon all who reject Christ as well as judgment on the heavens and the earth because of sin.

What should this mean to you? If you have never definitely invited Jesus Christ to come into your life, you should do it immediately. There is no second chance after death. Were you to die today your body would return to dust but your soul would go to hell. At the time of the Great White Throne judgment your body will be resurrected to be joined with your soul to stand before God in judgment. Following the judgment, both body and soul will be cast into hell forever. You may not believe this. You may flatly reject everything that is said in the Word of God relative to judgment. But your thoughts or attitude about the subject will not alter God's eternal truth in any way. What God has declared and written will remain throughout eternity. It is of utmost importance that you come to Christ now. Consider His words, "Come unto Me, all ye that labour and are heavy laden, and I will give you rest. Take My yoke upon you, and learn of Me; for I am meek and lowly in heart: and ye shall find rest unto your souls. For My yoke is easy, and My burden is light" (Matthew 11:28-30). Here is a gracious invitation from the Son of God. He calls upon you to lay upon Him the burden of your sins, that you might find rest for your soul. Heed this gracious invitation before it is too late.

Maybe you have been too busy to think about God. You are so occupied with the matters of this world, which to you seem to be of immediate importance. Maybe you are more interested in making money and accumulating a sizable bank account than you are in preparing for eternity. When it comes time to leave this world, you will find that all your riches will be meaningless. When you die, you will leave your riches behind. God says in 1 Timothy 6:7, "For we brought nothing into this world, and it is certain we can carry nothing out."

Years ago some men went to Alaska seeking gold. They went far into the interior. One day they came upon a miner's hut. It seemed to be as quiet as a grave. Entering the hut they found the skeletons of two men and a large quantity of gold. On a rough table in the hut was a letter. It told about their successful hunt for gold. When they found the gold they were so eager to get it that they forgot about the early coming of winter. Each day they found more gold. The fall passed by. Winter approached. One morning the men awoke to find a great snow storm upon them. For days the snow fell. It became deeper and deeper. Soon there was no hope of escape. All the food was used up. Then the men lay down and died in the midst of their gold. The two miners had coveted gold. Their only thought was to get more gold. They forgot to provide for the coming of the winter in that far north land.

Today there are many who covet gold and the perishing things of this world. They want money, houses, and land. They neglect to prepare for Heaven. How foolish it is to covet the things which perish and pass away; to live for this world and forget to prepare for the coming world! Do not make this mistake. Turn to Christ now. For be assured, even though it appears as though "all things continue as they were from the beginning of the creation," God declares that "the heavens and the earth, which are now, by the same word are kept in store, reserved unto fire against the day of judgment and perdition of ungodly men." Judgment is approaching quickly and after judgment, eternal hell. Are you ready to meet God? Have you believed on Christ? If not, receive Him into your heart before it is too late.

18.

REPUDIATION

"But, beloved, be not ignorant of this one thing, that one day is with the Lord as a thousand years, and a thousand years as one day. The Lord is not slack concerning His promise, as some men count slackness; but is longsuffering to usward, not willing that any should perish, but that all should come to repentance. But the day of the Lord will come as a thief in the night; in the which the heavens shall pass away with a great noise, and the elements shall melt with fervent heat, the earth also and the works that are therein shall be burned up. Seeing then that all these things shall be dissolved, what manner of persons ought ye to be in all holy conversation and godliness. Looking for and hasting unto the coming of the day of God, wherein the heavens being on fire shall be dissolved, and the elements shall melt with fervent heat?"—2 Peter 3:8-12

The false teachers had argued that since thousands of years had transpired without any unusual intervention by God, it would be unreasonable to expect such a rare phenomenon as the visible, bodily return of Christ. Peter reminded them of the flood during the time of Noah, proving that there has been at least one mighty intervention by God in the normal course of His care and preservation of creation. It is quite obvious that, if God interrupted the ordinary order of civilization once, He could do it again.

The apostle continues by repudiating the false claims of those who were seeking to castigate the truth of Christ's return. He informs them that they are not to be "ignorant of this one thing, that one day is with the Lord as a thousand years, and a thousand years as one day." Time is relative with God. He is not bound by it; He is the Creator of it. Humans are the subjects of time, but with the Lord one day is as a thousand years and a thousand years as one day.

Though He does not act according to human standards of time, nevertheless God is guided by His own wisdom in all things. Peter assures us that "the Lord is not slack concerning His promise, as some men count slackness." As it is used here "slackness" means "tardiness." God has promised in His Word that Christ will return. He has not told us when He will return, but in the providence of God the time is set. The Lord Jesus will not in any sense of the word be late or tardy when He appears. He will come at the exact moment of God's choosing.

The reason for the delay is revealed in the fact that God "is longsuffering . . . not willing that any should perish, but that all should come to repentance." Christ has not returned as yet because of the grace and mercy of our loving God. When Christ returns to the earth, judgment will be meted out upon all unbelievers. Paul makes this fact clear in 2 Thessalonians 1:7-9, "And to you who are troubled rest with us, when the Lord Jesus shall be revealed from heaven with His mighty angels, In flaming fire taking vengeance on them that know not God, and that obey not the gospel of our Lord Jesus Christ: Who shall be punished with everlasting destruction from the presence of the Lord, and from the glory of His power." There are unsaved millions who at this moment can be thankful that Christ has not come back as yet, for when He returns, they will be judged for their sins.

It is not God's desire that His creatures be judged for sin and cast into perdition. He is "longsuffering." In the *Amplified New Testament* this word is translated "extraordinarily patient." All of us deserve hell, but our God, because of His great love, is "extraordinarily patient." In Ezekiel 33:11 He says, "I have no pleasure in the death of the wicked." In Luke 13:34 we sense His tender love as He pleads with unbelieving Jews to come to Him: "O Jerusalem, Jerusalem, which killest the prophets, and stonest them that are sent unto thee; how often would I have gathered thy children together, as a hen doth gather her brood under her wings, and ye would not!" In the same manner in which these Jews turned their faces from the Lord, so thousands upon thousands of people all around the world are rejecting Him today. Many are too busy for God, indifferent to the claims of the Lord on their souls. God still loves them and longs for them to come to Him. But in spite of all He has done for them, many are still rejecting Him. There is probably no greater sin in all the universe than that of spurning the love of God.

A mother, in a tender moment, drew her two-year-old daughter to her and said, "Oh, I love you." The little girl was very much occupied with what she was doing at the moment and drew away saying, "Yes, I know." It was love taken for granted. What a tragedy it is when one hears the voice of God saying as He does from Calvary and from a thousand circumstances of life: "My child, I love you; I gave my Son to die for you; I shed my blood for you," only to answer with a nonchalance which shows that His love is ignored. Most of life's sadness and misery flows from such an attitude. Hear God's voice pleading with you to-day, confirming His love toward you. Have you returned this love to Him by believing on His Son? Do not look for another way. There is no other approach to God but through Jesus, His beloved Son.

Some time ago a busy merchant was led to see himself as a sinner. This conviction prompted him to seek for a savior. He earnestly desired to have his sins forgiven. He started going to church, feeling that such a practice would help to banish from his mind the thoughts of his sins. One day he heard a poor, blind man standing on a street corner reciting the Word of God aloud. The words he heard were those of Acts 4:12: "Neither is there salvation in any other: for there is none other name under heaven given among men, whereby we must be saved." As the merchant went on his way, those words kept ringing in his ears, "None other name, none other name." Later he said to himself, "I have been trying to save myself, thinking that praying, reading my Bible, and going to church would be sufficient. But it is only Jesus who can save." With the simple faith of a little child, this merchant came to Christ and was gloriously transformed by the power of God. Immediately he understood all about God's great love in providing a sin-bearer and a Saviour for him. Have you learned this simple lesson, this great truth of the Scriptures? God loves you today. He does not want you to die in your sins. He is desirous that you have life. Come to Him now before it is too late.

Men may procrastinate, they may even ridicule the doctrine of the return of Christ, as did the false teachers. But Peter discloses that irrespective of the attitude or the teachings of the unsaved, "the day of the Lord will come as a thief in the night; in the which the heavens shall pass away with a great noise, and the elements shall melt with fervent heat, the earth also and the works that are therein shall be burned up." "The day of the Lord" comprehends a whole series of tremendous events beginning with the premillennial return of Christ and continuing until the creation of the "new heavens and a new earth." The entire course is to cover a period of time of at least a thousand years. At the end of this millennium a great cataclysmic disturbance will transpire, resulting in the purging of the earth by fire, renovating it for the dwelling place of the people of God throughout eternity. All that man has produced through years of stress and toil will be completely destroyed as part of the preparation of the earth for the eternal habitation of the redeemed of the Lord.

Christ will come "as a thief in the night" in the sense that the time of His Coming is unknown. The Lord Jesus said in Luke 12:39: "And this know, that if the goodman of the house had known what hour the thief would come, he would have watched, and not have suffered his house to be broken through. Be ye therefore ready also: for the Son of man cometh at an hour when ye think not." Our Lord further says in Mark 13:32, "But of that day and that hour knoweth no man, no, not the angels which are in heaven, neither the Son, but the Father."

Though the time is not known, God has revealed certain signs in His Word whereby His people may know that the Coming of the Lord is near. We read in Luke 21:25-28: "And there shall be signs in the sun, and in the moon, and in the stars; and upon the earth distress of nations, with perplexity; the sea and the waves roaring; Men's hearts failing them for fear, and for looking after those things which are coming on the earth: for the powers of heaven shall be shaken. And then shall they see the Son of man coming in a cloud with power and great glory. And when these things begin to come to pass, then look up, and lift up your heads; for your redemption draweth nigh."

Has there ever been a time in history when there was more "distress of nations" than at the present time? The entire world is in turmoil. The political leaders of practically every nation are bewildered and confused as they endeavor to keep abreast of the fast-moving events of the day. As a result, men's hearts are failing them for fear. In both the east and the west the characteristic mark of the age is "fear." God's Word makes it clear that all this is a sign of something else—"then shall they see the Son of man coming in a cloud with power and great glory." There can be no doubt about it. The return of Christ is near at hand. He is coming! He is coming soon! His Coming will be unannounced. He will come "as a thief in the night." When He appears, if you do not know Him as Lord, you must face Him as your judge. How important it is that you come to Him now if you have not already done so.

On a certain Monday at Port Chicago several years ago, there seemed nothing particularly unusual about the day. In the morning the war workers had rushed to their various shifts, and then, work finished, they trudged wearily homeward. Life continued as it did every Monday in Port Chicago until at exactly 10:19 P.M. there was a rumble and a roar that was heard for many miles around. Two ammunition ships had exploded. According to navy pilots, flames shot nearly two miles in the air. So great was the blast that windows rattled and buildings shook even in San Francisco, thirty miles away. The earth trembled for fifty miles in every direction. Buildings were blown to matchwood and not one in the town of Port Chicago was left intact. Homes were ruined; stores were in shambles; scores of people were injured. The entire town of fifteen hundred people was plunged into chaos without water, electricity, or gas. In an instant a prosperous city was leveled to worthless debris. In ten horrible seconds more than three hundred humans ceased to exist on earth. Naturally, no one expected this catastrophe. Had any indication of it been given, every precaution would have been taken to prevent it; if it could not have been prevented, the city would have been evacuated. But it came unannounced. There was no warning of any kind.

The Lord Jesus will come in the same surprising manner. Doubtless men will be at work as usual, their wives fulfilling the duties of the home, their children in school. The minds of most people will be crowded with the thoughts and cares of this life. Suddenly the Son of God will return to earth as He said He would. Millions will be wholly unprepared for His return.

The same was true at the time of the flood. God sent Noah to the people to warn and prepare them. Instead of responding to the call of God through His servant, they laughed at him and ridiculed his preaching. At God's appointed time, the rains began to fall and soon the whole earth was engulfed in the heaven-sent deluge. The return of Christ will be equally unexpected; "As the days of Noah were, so shall also the coming of the Son of man be" (Matthew 24:37).

The important question is not, will the Lord come? Peter assures us of this fact. But how do we stand in our personal relationship to the Lord? Will we be *ready* to meet Him when He comes? "Seeing then that all these things shall be dissolved, what manner of persons ought ye to be in all holy conversation and godliness, Looking for and hasting unto the coming of the day of God, wherein the heavens being on fire shall be dissolved and the elements shall melt with fervent heat." There are two obligations expressed here that are incumbent upon all born-again believers relative to the Second Coming—holiness and evangelism.

Those of God's people who firmly believe the Scriptures in regard to the truth of Christ's return will prove their belief by lives of holiness. "For the grace of God that bringeth salvation hath appeared to all men, Teaching us that, denying ungodliness and worldly lusts, we should live soberly, righteously, and godly, in this present world; Looking for that blessed hope, and the glorious appearing of the great God and our Saviour Jesus Christ" (Titus 2:11-13). Those who are looking for their Lord will desire to be like Him even now. Assuredly we shall be transformed into His perfection when He does come. We shall be sinless and pure, even as He is. But anticipating His return, we should be drawing on His power to live an effectual life of holiness and obedience at this very moment. The same power that will make us like unto His glorious image is available now to enable us to walk in the light as He is in the light.

Is it not true that many of God's dear people are playing with sin rather than abhoring it and resisting it. They enjoy it and cling to it, even though they profess to be followers of the Lord Jesus Christ. The real tragedy of the matter is seen in the results in their lives: no joy; no peace; worst of all, no fruit. In these days of loose morals, godless talk, and wickedness of all sorts, how important it is that every believer keep his eyes fixed on Christ, for sin is very alluring. The devil makes it attractive and appealing, but the end is ruinous.

I am told that in some parts of the world there is a tree which has been named the Judas tree because of its deceitfulness. This tree, it is said, has beautiful crimson blossoms which appear prior to its leaves. Their flaming beauty attracts innumerable insects. The busy bee, ever on the lookout for honey, is drawn to the flower. But every insect and every bee that alights upon the blossoms imbibes a fatal opiate and drops dead among the crimson blossoms. Below the Judas tree lie scores of lifeless victims.

How descriptively this tree pictures the deceitfulness and dangers of sin. Even with the best of intentions, one may meet disaster by yielding to sin. Only the wisdom and the power of the Holy Spirit can enable us to discern between good and evil, between the true and the false. It is for this reason that we should surrender ourselves to Christ completely, following Him closely in lives of holiness. To every believer, God's voice speaks clearly, "Ye shall therefore be holy, for I am holy" (Leviticus 11:45).

Not only should the hope of the return of Christ prompt the believer to holiness. It should inspire and motivate him to sacrifice to spread the gospel to every lost soul who has never yet heard of redemption through the Saviour. Peter says "looking for and hasting unto the coming of the day of God." The word "hasting" as used here can mean "hastening onward the day of God." This is not to suggest that God's time is changeable, but rather that He appoints His people as instruments in accomplishing the events which precede the day of the Lord. We are to pray for His Coming and at the same time we are to bear witness to Christ to the peoples of all nations.

When Christ returns He will expect to find us working for Him. In Matthew 24:45-46 He says: "Who then is a faithful and wise servant, whom his lord hath made ruler over his household, to give them meat in due season? Blessed is that servant, whom his lord when he cometh shall find so doing." We are to be busy giving out the Bread of Life to those who are spiritually destitute. It is the doctrine of the return of Christ that should challenge us above all else to seek the lost for Christ. Usually, those who are looking for His return are soul-winners. They are living for the purpose of leading lost and dying souls to the Saviour. The return of Christ is more than a study topic; it is a call to the army of God to march, to act, to evangelize.

Years ago Alexander Duff, the veteran missionary to India, went home to Scotland to die. In great feebleness he appeared before the Scotch Presbyterian assembly and pleaded for missionaries for India. In the midst of his appeal he fainted and was taken into another room. After physicians had worked over him for some time he finally recovered consciousness. When he realized where he was, he said, "I didn't finish my appeal. Take me back and let me finish it." But they told him he could do it only at the peril of his life. He said, "I'll do it if I die." So they led the white-haired veteran back into the assembly hall. As he appeared at the door, those present sprang to their feet as one man to greet him, and listened in tearful and breathless silence to the grand old hero of the cross.

"Fathers and mothers of Scotland, is it true that you have no more sons to send to India?" he asked with trembling voice. "There is money in the bank to send them, but where are the laborers who will go into the field? When Queen Victoria calls for volunteers for her army in India, you freely give your sons and say nothing about the trying climate of that land. But when the Lord Jesus calls for volunteers you say, 'We have no more sons to give.'" Then turning to the moderator of the assembly he said, "Mr. Moderator, if it is true that Scotland has no more sons to give to Christ for India, then, although I lost my health in that land and came home to die, I will be off tomorrow and go back to the shores of the Ganges and lay my life down as a witness for Christ, to let India's millions know that there is at least one Scotsman who is ready to die for them."

Why did Alexander Duff act so? What was it that made him create such a scene? He was a man with a burden and a vision, who believed in the return of his Lord; because he believed in Christ's return, he believed that he should be watching and working. The burden of India's perishing millions lay heavily upon him. He had a responsibility to a soon-coming Christ. How then could he live for himself?

Do we really believe that Christ will return as the Bible declares? If so, it means that we who know Christ will commit ourselves fully to the will and the work of the Lord, that in these days of gross wickedness and rank unbelief we shall be instruments of holiness and power in the hands of a mighty God.

If you do not know the Lord you should seek Him immediately, realizing that the Coming of Christ draweth nigh. He is willing to save all who come to Him, but you must come. Have you come? Heed God's gracious invitation, "Ho, every one that thirsteth, come ye to the waters, and he that hath no money; come ye, buy, and eat; yea, come, buy wine and milk without money and without price" (Isaiah 55:1).

19.

RENOVATION

"Nevertheless we, according to His promise, look for new heavens and a new earth, wherein dwelleth righteousness. Wherefore, beloved, seeing that ye look for such things, be diligent that ye may be found of Him in peace, without spot, and blameless."—2 Peter 3:13-14

Following the great conflagration which will purge the heavens and the earth of all evil and wickedness, the "new heavens and a new earth" will emerge "wherein dwelleth righteousness." The heavens and the earth will be completely renovated and prepared for the people of God, possibly appearing somewhat like the Garden of Eden in beauty and perfection. We may be assured that this prophecy is not based upon vain speculation, but as Peter says, it is "according to His promise." Doubtless the apostle is referring to God's promise found in Isaiah 65:17, "For, behold, I create new heavens and a new earth: and the former shall not be remembered, nor come into mind."

Have you ever wondered why it will be necessary for God to purge the heavens? Is there iniquity in heaven?

The Scriptures reveal the fact of three heavens: the upper air where the birds fly, the region in which the stars revolve, and the abode of Christ's human nature with the spirits of the departed saints, known as Paradise. In Ephesians 2:2 we read that Satan is "the prince of the power of the air." Further on in chapter 6 of this same Epistle Paul tells us that "we wrestle not against flesh and blood, but against principalities, against powers, against the rulers of the darkness of this world, against spiritual wickedness in high places" (Ephesians 6:12). It is quite obvious from these verses that Satan and millions of fallen angels inhabit the heavens, not Paradise where Christ and His saints dwell, but the first and second heavens. Thus, wherever Satan has been at work will need cleansing from sin. The third Heaven, the dwelling place of Christ, has not been tainted by the evil one. Before his fall the devil was one of God's holy angels. But upon his refusal to obey God, he was immediately expelled from the Lord's presence. The earth and the air became the devil's sphere of operation, where he continues as the elusive and crafty deceiver. Thus, it would seem that it will be the first and second heavens only that are purged and renovated along with the earth.

Peter reveals that we are to look for "new heavens and a new earth, wherein dwelleth righteousness." The heavens and earth are to be "new" in the sense of being renewed and restored, not recreated. They will be the same heavens and earth purified, glorified, and redeemed. Following the restoration, the earth will become the scene of righteousness, blessedness, and celestial peace as opposed to wickedness, unhappiness, and universal unrest. The present heavens, and the earth, as beautiful as they are, are under the curse as the result of Adam's transgression. All of creation awaits redemption, or perfecting. Paul makes this fact clear in Romans 8:22-23: "For we know that the whole creation groaneth and travaileth in pain together until now. And not only they, but ourselves also, which have the firstfruits of the Spirit, even we ourselves groan within ourselves, waiting for the adoption, to wit, the redemption of our body."

The new earth will be the dwelling place for the saints of God throughout all eternity. The last two chapters of the Bible give a clear and descriptive picture of what this habitation will be like. In Revelation 21:1,2-5 the Apostle John writes, "And I saw a new heaven and a new earth: for the first heaven and the first earth were passed away. . . . And I heard a great voice out of heaven saying, Behold, the tabernacle of God is with men, and He will dwell with them, and they shall be His people, and God Himself shall be with them, and be their God. And God shall wipe away all tears from their eyes; and there shall be no more death, neither sorrow, nor crying, neither shall there be any more pain: for the former things are passed away. And He that sat upon the throne said, Behold, I make all things new. And He said unto me, Write: for these words are true and faithful."

What a wonderful place this will be! Are you going there? Will you see it? Not everyone will. In this same chapter in which God depicts the glories of the new heavens and new earth, He also says, "But the fearful, and unbelieving, and the abominable, and murderers, and whoremongers, and sorcerers, and idolaters, and all liars, shall have their part in the lake which burneth with fire and brimstone: which is the second death" (Revelation 21:8). No, not everyone will dwell in the new heavens and the new earth. Only those will be there who have received the Lord Jesus Christ into their hearts during their lifetime in this world. Everyone else will spend eternity in hell. The Bible makes this very plain. Either we shall be with Christ or forever separated from Him.

If there is any uncertainty in your heart about going to Heaven, make sure of your entrance now. Believe on the Lord Jesus Christ, God's beloved Son, and as the Scripture says, immediately you will be "passed from death unto life" (John 5:24).

Could it be that you are so occupied with the cares of this present world that you have little concern about Heaven? It may be that you are like a church member who listened to her pastor preach on the subject of Heaven one Sunday. After the service, in speaking to him, she said, "Pastor, I never heard a sermon on Heaven before, and I must confess I am not very much interested. That sounds awful for a church member to say, doesn't it?" The pastor thought to himself, "I believe this woman is depending on her church membership for her salvation. I must see her further about this." But before he had time to call on the woman, her five-year-old daughter died.

Immediately the pastor went to her home. The mother was quite broken up and greatly distressed. Almost hysterical, she said to the pastor, "Oh, I can't understand why God allowed her to die. I prayed so hard that she would get better." After offering words of comfort the minister seized the opportunity and said, "Not long ago you told me you weren't interested in Heaven. Perhaps God has taken your treasure from you so that you will become interested and want to follow your loved one into Heaven. Do you really know Christ as your Saviour and Lord?" he asked. She admitted that though she was a church member she had never really received Christ. There in the environs of that death-saddened home, the pastor led one of his church members to a saving knowledge of Jesus Christ. Immediately Heaven became a reality to her, not only because of a precious daughter she would meet again someday, but because Christ is there.

Possibly you have loved ones in Heaven. Will you meet them there? Surely you want to spend eternity with them in the presence of our wonderful Lord. He has told us the way in His Word. The decision rests with you. Receive Christ into your heart and be assured of eternity with him.

Though the Lord has given a lucid picture in Revelation 21 and 22 of what the new heavens and new earth will be like, it is impossible for us to have a complete understanding because of the limitations of communication. Divine truth can only be known in terms of human experience. Throughout the Scripture God has revealed to us things we have not seen or experienced in language that we can understand. Doubtless Heaven will be far more wonderful than that which is revealed in the Book of the Revelation. But in our present state we are not able to comprehend more than we have seen or known.

Dr. William Edward Biederwolf used to tell of a little girl who was blind from birth and who knew only the beauties of earth as told by her mother's lips. A noted surgeon performed an operation on her eyes, which after many weeks proved successful. As the last bandage dropped away she flew into her mother's arms and then to the windows, and as the glories of earth rolled into her vision she turned to her mother and said, "Oh, Mama, why didn't you tell me it was so beautiful?" The mother wiped away the tears of joy and said, "My precious child, I tried to tell you but I couldn't do it."

When the Lord's people catch their first glimpse of the enrapturing and exquisite beauty of the new heavens and the new earth, I think they will say to John the Apostle, "John, why didn't you tell us it was so wonderful?" Probably John will reply, "I tried to tell you in chapters 21 and 22 of the last book in the Bible, but I couldn't do it." There are not enough words in the English language to describe the grandeur and magnificence of Heaven. In 1 Corinthians 2:9-10 we read: "Eye hath not seen, nor ear heard, neither have entered into the heart of man, the things which God hath prepared for them that love Him. But God hath revealed them unto us by His Spirit: for the Spirit searcheth all things, yea, the deep things of God." Paul assures us that the Lord has revealed to His own blood-bought children all that can possibly be known now about Heaven and the future. But there is so much we shall not know and cannot know until we meet Christ face to face and become like Him.

To me, one of the most heartening and consoling statements in the Bible relative to Heaven is found in Hebrews 4:9: "There remaineth therefore a rest to the people of God." Most of us have spent long years of toil on this earth, years that have been interspersed with many hardships and trials. But oh, the joy and confidence of knowing that "There remaineth therefore a rest to the people of God." It is wonderful to be a Christian. In fact, we wonder how people can live without Christ amidst the perplexing problems and disturbing cares of this life. For the true believer, the best is yet to come. The words of the prophet are so appropriate, "Arise ye, and depart; for this is not your rest" (Micah 2:10). God's people enter the promised rest of Christ immediately upon heeding His invitation of Matthew 11:28, "Come unto Me, all ye that labor and are heavy laden, and I will give you rest." Our present rest, wonderful as it is, is only a foretaste of that which we shall soon experience throughout eternity in the presence of our loving Lord.

One night, years ago, a forest fire was raging in a southern wilderness. A tribe of Indians was driven on and on, and after many hours of weary trudging and travel through dense brush and forest they came to a spreading river. They plunged into the water and, after reaching the other bank, the old chief stuck his tent pole into the ground, threw himself on the grass, and cried, "Alabama" —the Indian word for "here we may rest." But the old chief was not a prophet. They were in the vicinity of a hostile tribe and soon were surrounded by foes more relentless than the forest fire. Where they looked for rest and the delight of a home, they found only the quiet of a grave. Actually, earth has no "alabama" for the soul. But, praise God, there is one soon to come. "Nevertheless we, according to His promise, look for new heavens and a new earth, wherein dwelleth righteousness."

This marvelous hope of the new heavens and the new earth should inspire every true believer to the fulfillment of present responsibility. The Bible is an intensely practical book. In the Scriptures, rarely do we find a message of hope for the future without a subsequent challenge to a full and complete commitment to our immediate obligations. Thus Peter says, "Wherefore, beloved, seeing that ye look for such things, be diligent that ye may be found of Him in peace, without spot, and blameless." If we are possessors of the "blessed hope," this fact should motivate us to faithfulness in the performance of the duties outlined for us in the Word of God. Peter mentions a few of them in this verse.

Notice the first—"that ye may be found of Him in peace." It would seem that the Spirit of God speaking through the apostle is revealing several things here. With the realization of the soon return of Christ and the impending events in connection with His return, there is an immediate call for all who are unsaved to enter into peace with God immediately. One does not *make peace* with God, but rather he receives the peace God has already made and provided through the sacrifice of His Son on the cross: "And having made peace through the blood of His cross, by Him to reconcile all things unto Himself; by Him, I say, whether they be things in earth, or things in heaven" (Colossians 1:20). Eternal peace becomes the instantaneous possession of all who sincerely believe on the Lord Jesus Christ. Apart from Him, God's peace cannot be known. Thousands upon thousands of people are miserable and wretched today because they know nothing of God's wonderful peace, received by believing on the Lord Jesus Christ.

To be sure, the devil is capitalizing on the millions of

restless and disturbed hearts and minds devoid of God's peace. One of our well-read magazines has exposed the "psycho-phonies" who are preying on the mentally upset and relieving them of half a billion dollars yearly. More than twenty-five thousand "phony" psychologists are giving dangerous and bad advice to people in trouble today. Dr. Fillmore H. Sanford, then executive secretary of the American Psychological Association, was said to have estimated the phonies' annual intake as high as $375,000,000 yearly and possibly over half a billion dollars. "At its conservative low, it equals about five per cent of the amount spent each year in this country for all medical care.

"This sum is not just wasted money, harmlessly spent for foolish or useless counseling. There are 8,500,000 psychiatric cases in the United States. More than 200,000 new patients are admitted to mental hospitals each year. No one knows exactly how many of these have been shoved across the border of what the law calls insanity by the callous or ignorant 'psycho-phonies' who are operating free of all legal restraint in nearly all of our major cities."

The article cited the case of a California husband and wife who were quarreling bitterly, and picked a "psychologist" from the phone book. His splashy advertisement was impressive and they were willing to try whatever he advised. He told them they were sexually mismated and suggested that they prove it to their own satisfaction by taking other partners. They did, and during the next six months each drifted through a series of shoddy affairs under the supervision of their "doctor." As a result, the wife is in a mental institution, the husband disappeared, and their three-year-old child had to be placed in a foster home.

Isn't it sad that someone could not have told these parents that without the peace one finds in the Lord by believing on Christ, there is no peace to be found. Should it be that you are not a recipient of this peace, turn to Christ and receive Him immediately. What Isaiah wrote thousands of years ago will suddenly become a reality in your life: "Thou wilt keep him in perfect peace, whose mind is stayed on Thee; because he trusteth in Thee" (Isaiah 26:3).

It should also be realized that it is possible for one to have peace *with God* without enjoying the peace *of God*. As simply as we appropriated salvation by believing on Christ, we must accept God's peace daily as His gift to sustain us amidst the trials and difficulties of life. There are no limits to the peace which God will give to those who love Him. It is possible to live free from stress and worry; the only reason we do not is because we fail to take God at His Word by constantly receiving of His fullness and, as a result, His peace. Paul says in Philippians 4:6-7: "Be careful for nothing; but in every thing by prayer and supplication with thanksgiving let your requests be made known unto God. And the peace of God, which passeth all understanding, shall keep your hearts and minds through Christ Jesus."

Some years ago Jeanette Vellman sat in her office in a mission hospital when suddenly there came a rapid, insistent knock at the door. Quickly she opened it. There stood Po-hong, a third-year student nurse, her face showing fear and distrust. Before either of them got to a chair the student nurse burst out, "I've done an awful thing, Miss

Vellman, an awful thing." She went on to relate with hurry and great difficulty that a baby had tipped off the scales while she was weighing him. No, she hadn't left him. Yes, the doctor had already seen him. He wasn't hurt, for he had only rolled to the top of the table on which the scales stood.

Miss Vellman could not minimize the student nurse's mistake, but quietly she commented that she was happy and thankful that the baby was all right. She added that she was certain that Po-hong would not let it happen again and that she would continue to trust her. There was no reprimand, no excitement on Miss Vellman's part, but with kindness she comforted the distressed student.

Days passed into weeks. Then one day Po-hung went to the nurse's office to see Miss Vellman. This visit to the nurse's office was quite different from the former. Po-hong was more gentle, less scornful, very congenial. Her opening words were, "I now believe in Christ and Christians. Do you know why?" Miss Vellman had talked to her many times about our Saviour. She had prayed with her, but Po-hong had given few signs of interest.

"Why?" asked Miss Vellman.

"Do you remember the day I came to see you about the mistake I made? I was terribly frightened and worried, but you were calm and peaceful and showed only a loving and understanding heart. I knew then that there was something to being a Christian—and now I am one, too." Miss Vellman's eyes suddenly became moist, her throat dry. Standing to her feet, she took Po-hung's hand, saying in Chinese, "I am glad you have found peace for your heart. God bless you." They had prayer together, but after Po-hong left Miss Vellman went to her knees, thanking God for the peace He gives for every circumstance of life. Miss Vellman is one believer who knows not only peace *with* God but the peace *of* God. Is His peace your possession?

Not only are those who possess the "blessed hope" expected to enjoy God's wonderful peace, they are to live "without spot . . . blameless." Actually, Heaven begins within our hearts the moment Christ comes in. It is for this reason that we should permit Him to live through us, producing lives that are well pleasing in His sight. Only as we yield to His control is it possible to live "without spot" and to be "blameless." It should never be forgotten that we are God's "workmanship, created in Christ Jesus unto good works, which God has before ordained that we should walk in them" (Ephesians 2:10). Not only are we God's workmanship by virtue of the fact that He saved us, but we should be His workmanship in every step we take in our Christian experience. If we are to live victoriously, "without spot and blameless," there must be a complete moment-by-moment dependence on Him.

In anticipation of our soon-coming Lord, is your spiritual life what it should be if Christ were to return today? Are you living today as you would have Him find you when He comes? Are there little sins and habits in your life that would grieve Him? Well, He is coming! Soon we must face Him. Let us be ready. "Wherefore, beloved, seeing that ye look for such things," let us surrender our entire selves to His Lordship and control.

If you are not one of His own, if you cannot say Christ is "my" Lord, at this very moment ask Him to come into your heart. Do not delay. He is ready. What about you?

20.

REGENERATION

"And account that the longsuffering of our Lord is salvation;
even as our beloved brother Paul also according to the wisdom
given unto him hath written unto you; As also in all his
epistles, speaking in them of these things; in which are some
things hard to be understood, which they that are unlearned
and unstable wrest, as they do also the other scriptures, unto
their own destruction."—2 Peter 3:15-16

With clarity and certainty Peter has been stressing the
fact of future judgment on all unbelievers and all of creation. Thousands of centuries have passed and still this
prophesied judgment has not come. Some may wonder as
to the cause of the delay. Peter gives the fundamental reason as he says, "And account that the longsuffering of our
Lord is salvation." God's slowness in avenging His wrath
for sin is because He is "not willing that any should perish, but that all should come to repentance" (2 Peter 3:9).
He is giving the unsaved every possible opportunity to
repent and be saved before it is too late.

The only appointed means God has given whereby lost

men and women might be saved is regeneration, the new birth. Regeneration is an act of God's free grace, whereby one who believes in the atoning work of Jesus Christ is divinely quickened and made the recipient of a new nature. Without this divine quickening there is no forgiveness for sin. The end result is judgment. Because of His great love and concern for the souls of men, God is forestalling His judgment in order that the lost might turn to Him and be born again.

The Lord Jesus said in John 3:5, "Except a man be born of water and of the Spirit, he cannot enter into the kingdom of God." The "water" refers to God's Word as it is revealed in the Bible; and the Spirit, of course, is the Holy Spirit, the third person of the Trinity. The Word is the medium God uses to unfold the way of salvation. The Holy Spirit is the agency He uses to apply the truth and to impart new life to those who are willing to believe in Christ. There is no excuse for anyone who has a copy of the Bible to say that he cannot know the way. If one will read the Scripture with a desire to understand its message, the Spirit of God will make the message clear. If one receives the message of salvation through Christ by sincerely believing on Him, the Holy Spirit will give new life immediately.

The Apostle Paul, in writing to the Ephesians, portrays the past, present, and future of the believer who has been regenerated by the Spirit of God. First, he describes the past in Ephesians 2:1-3, portraying the believer as seen before his new birth without regard of any kind toward God and His righteousness: "And you hath He quickened, who were dead in trespasses and sins; Wherein in time past ye walked according to the course of this world, according to the prince of the power of the air, the spirit that now worketh in the children of disobedience: Among whom also we all had our conversation in times past in the lusts of our flesh, fulfilling the desires of the flesh and of the mind; and were by nature the children of wrath, even as others." Next notice the believer's present, in verses 4-6: "But God, who is rich in mercy, for His great love wherewith He loved us, Even when we were dead in sins, hath quickened us together with Christ, (by grace ye are saved;) And hath raised us up together, and made us sit together in heavenly places in Christ Jesus." Here we see the divine quickening or the new birth which results immediately, the moment one believes on Christ. The believer is made "a new creature: old things are passed away; behold, all things are become new" (2 Corinthians 5:17). At the same time the child of God experiences a spiritual resurrection enabling him to walk in a manner well-pleasing to the Lord. It appears from verse 7, however, that the best is yet to come: "That in the ages to come He might show the exceeding riches of His grace in His kindness toward us through Christ Jesus." It is grand to be a Christian now. Surely anyone who has been genuinely saved would never desire to revert to the old ways of life. But how much more wonderful it will be throughout all of eternity as we fellowship with the living Christ enjoying "the exceeding riches of His grace in His kindness toward us."

Lest anyone should think he can save himself, let it be understood that the new birth is a miracle. Only God can perform miracles. There is a sense in which modern industry is working apparent miracles. Men extract the ultra-lightweight metal magnesium from sea water. The chemical industry turns soybeans into paint, natural gas into television cabinets, and coal into shower curtains. The chemist can take apart, molecule by molecule, various forms of matter, and put them together again to form entirely new substances not found in nature. He can duplicate synthetically many of the fine creations of nature. He can transform ordinary substances into myriads of new and useful forms. From hydrocarbons alone the chemical industry now produces over fifty thousand compounds. But our modern magic lies defeated and helpless before man himself. Neither chemistry nor surgery can change a sinner's hardened heart, nor put love, mercy, and peace into the flinty soul of the ungodly. Only the grace of God as revealed in Jesus Christ can miraculously transform the sinner into a saint.

Modern research has been able to give people radio programs, but not righteousness; television, but not spiritual vision; automobiles, but not the self-restraint to drive them safely; liberty, but not discipline; knowledge, but not wisdom; entertainment, but not inner peace; pleasure, but not love for God; wine, women, and song, but not purity and holiness. People would be a million times better off if they had fewer material things and a more sincere desire to know and do the will of God. The need of our day is fewer counterfeit and synthetic substitutes for satisfaction and more genuine conversions to Christ and His great love.

Judgment is sure to come. The Bible reveals this fact with unequivocal certitude. God says in Hebrews 9:27,

"It is appointed unto men once to die, but after this the judgment." Let no unsaved person deceive himself into thinking that by some man-made attempt he can escape the judgment of God. The fact that God has not yet brought the unsaved to judgment is an unquestionable proof of His unlimited grace and mercy. Few of us have an adequate understanding of God's unfathomable love. In 1 John 4:10 we read: "Herein is love, not that we loved God, but that He loved us, and sent His Son to be the propitiation for our sins." Had it not been for His matchless grace prompting Him to take the first step in making salvation possible, none of us could be saved. If you are not a child of God, you should come to the Lord because of His unfathomable love for you. It is not His will that you perish and go to an eternal hell. He wants you to believe on His beloved Son that you might have the best in this life, with the hope of an eternity to be spent with Him. Do not spurn God's love. Do not ignore His compassion for you. Receive new life through His Son, Jesus Christ.

A young son of a wealthy Christian man had become extremely wayward and extravagant in his habits. Finally, quarreling with his father because he had refused him all the money he demanded, he left home in anger and followed the paths of a reckless life. He went deeper and deeper into sin until, after spending all his money, he was desperate, willing to do anything to get more money. He heard that his father and mother were away from home for a time of extended travel. The boy said to himself, "My father owes me a living and I will have it." He broke into his parents' home. Knowing where the valuables were kept, he soon had access to them. Thumbing through some of the valuable papers, neatly tucked in a box he found his father's will. Curious, he read it—and to his utter astonishment he found his name among the heirs, with a large bequest set against it. At first, he could hardly believe what he saw. He could not believe that after the way he had treated his parents, his father still retained him in the will, giving him the same portion as the other brothers and sisters.

"Can it be," he said to himself, "that my father loves me in spite of all my bitterness and hatred toward him? Can it be that in spite of the shame I have brought upon him he is still ready to treat me as a son?" Such thoughts as these were the means of bringing the boy to repentance and reconciliation with his father. He had not dreamed that his father loved him so.

Maybe you have thought much the same way about God. Possibly you have felt that God has been angry with you, that He has permitted many things to come into your life to punish you. It is just the opposite. You are mistaken. He longs to embrace you and to assure you of His full and free forgiveness for all you have done, and to tell you of the inheritance which is waiting for you if only you will claim it through His beloved Son, Jesus Christ.

"But," you may reply, "I do not think that reconciliation with God is to be found as easily as that. Do you mean to say that I may believe that God loves me and because Christ died upon the cross for my sins I can be saved at this very moment?" That is exactly what I mean. God assures us of this in John 3:16: He "so loved the world," that is, the unbelievers and the ungodly, that He "gave His only begotten Son, that whosoever believeth in Him should not perish, but have everlasting life." He invites you to make full proof of this love by coming to Him now. If you will, He gives the indisputable promise in John 6:37, "Him that cometh to Me I will in no wise cast out."

Peter further tells us that he was not alone in the portrayal of this transforming message of God's love for sinners. He says that his "beloved brother Paul also according to the wisdom given unto him hath written unto you." One need not read far into any of Paul's Epistles without sensing the impact of a man burning with the zeal of the Lord. Impassioned by the Spirit of God, he presents the message of regeneration through the shed blood of Christ. Like Peter, the Apostle Paul upheld the name of Christ as the only way of salvation, "Therefore being justified by faith, we have peace with God through our Lord Jesus Christ" (Romans 5:1). He proclaimed this truth with a sense of urgency, beseeching lost men and women to make an immediate decision for the Lord, "Behold, now is the accepted time; behold, now is the day of salvation" (2 Corinthians 6:2). Also like Peter, he warns of the soon return of Christ and pleads with God's people for a complete commitment and surrender to the Saviour: "And that, knowing the time, that now it is high time to awake out of sleep: for now is our salvation nearer than when we believed. The night is far spent, the day is at hand: let us therefore cast off the works of darkness, and put on the armour of light" (Romans 13:11-12).

Peter further says concerning the record Paul has given of divine truth that in these writings there are "some things hard to be understood which they that are unlearned and unstable wrest, as they do also the other scriptures, unto their own destruction." Peter was not alone in his problems with the false teachers. Repeatedly, Paul was confronted by ungodly men whose minds were closed to the truth. The word "unlearned" which Peter uses to describe them does not mean that they were unscholarly or ignorant in worldly wisdom. Rather, they were blind to spiritual truth. Even though they tried to reason it out, they were devoid of spiritual understanding. Their unregenerate hearts would not permit them to comprehend the message of grace and redemption. This was not all. Peter tells us that they *wrested* the Scriptures; that is, they distorted and misinterpreted God's truth. Such handling of the Word of God can only produce catastrophe. Thus, the end result of this humanistic attempt to understand the Scriptures resulted in confusion, "For the preaching of the cross is to them that perish foolishness" (1 Corinthians 1:18).

The real problem of the false teachers who plagued both Peter and Paul was that they had never experienced the new birth. Even though they were brilliant and wise in the understanding of the philosophies of their day, they were wholly incapable of grasping the elementary truths of God's Word. Their condition is described clearly in 1 Corinthians 1:27-29: "But God hath chosen the foolish things of the world to confound the wise; and God hath chosen the weak things of the world to confound the things which are mighty; And base things of the world, and things which are despised, hath God chosen, yea and things which are not, to bring to nought things that are: That no flesh should glory in His presence."

No one will ever be able to boast that he found God or

understood spiritual truth on the basis of his own reasoning or rationalizing. There is only one universal approach to God. All must come the same way, whether a child or an adult, whether learned or uneducated, whether rich or poor. Jesus declared in John 3:7, "Marvel not that I said unto thee, Ye must be born again." Education, cultivation, reformation, training of the old nature will never turn flesh into spirit; "That which is born of the flesh is flesh" (John 3:6). It may be decent or indecent flesh, religious or irreligious, pious or profane, but it is still flesh. Nicodemus was a master of Israel. He was a wise man, well trained in the wisdom of the world. Yet, he had no understanding whatsoever of the new birth. This subject continues to baffle the most erudite and well-trained minds of our day.

Someone may be quick to remind us of the progress of man, especially in the last twenty-five or thirty years. Are not things on the upgrade? Consider the progress: sound and color movies, radio and television, metals, radar, plastics, electronics, drugs, air-conditioning, airplanes, space travel. Things have improved; but what about man? One need only consider organized crime, institutionalized murder, multitudes on the skid rows, corruption in government, the infiltration of godless communism, unnecessary and exhausting wars, vast armies of hopeless alcoholics, increasing juvenile delinquency, the persistence of disease in forms old and new. Progress? Yes, we have made some progress, but the heart of man is still as corrupt as ever. David's words of thousands of years ago are still descriptive of all who are born into this world, "Behold, I was shapen in iniquity; and in sin did my mother conceive me" (Psalm 51:5). Every baby enters this life born with the taint of sin inherited from his ancestral grandparent, Adam. The heart of man is no different from Adam's sinful heart of centuries before. Paul sums it up well as he says in 2 Timothy 3:13, "But evil men and seducers shall wax worse and worse, deceiving, and being deceived."

Man's only hope is regeneration—a new birth. If you have not already come to God, if you have not been born from above by believing on Christ, God desires that you come now. What He has declared in Peter's second Epistle is His eternal Word. The Lord Jesus will return. When He returns the wicked will be judged. After the judgment they will be cast into eternal hell. These are indubitable facts revealed in the Scriptures. They will never be changed. Believe them and come to the Saviour while you have the opportunity.

It is said that when the mighty *Titanic* sank on its maiden voyage to America, the scene outside the White Star office in Liverpool, England, was actually beyond description. A great crowd of the relatives and friends of those who had taken passage on that ill-fated vessel thronged the street and all traffic was suspended. On either side of the main entrance a large board had been placed. Above one was printed in large letters, "Known to be saved"; on the other, "Known to be lost." Every now and then a man would appear from the office bearing a piece of cardboard on which was written the name of one of the passengers. As he stood at the entrance and faced the crowd and held up the name, a deathly stillness swept over that vast audience. The people watched breathlessly to see to which of the boards he would pin the name.

Realize it: at this very moment you are either saved or lost. There is no middle ground. The crowd that stood outside the White Star office realized that there were but two classes among those who had traveled on that ship. There was no board for those who were neither saved nor lost. Likewise, there are only two divisions today. In which class are you? Be honest with yourself and with God. If you are lost, and if you should die in that state, you will be eternally lost. Don't gamble with time. Don't play with God. Hear His voice speaking to you at this moment, "Draw nigh to God, and He will draw nigh to you" (James 4:8). What could be fairer than this? If you are willing to open your heart to Him, He will immediately pour the blessings of eternity on your soul.

Possibly you have been so busy in caring for the affairs of this life that you have completely overlooked that of greater importance, the salvation of your soul. May I beseech you to pause amidst the busy hours to think about that of which you may never think again, the eternal salvation of your soul.

NO TIME FOR GOD

You've time to build houses, and in them to dwell,
   And time to do business—to buy and to sell,
But none for repentance, or deep, earnest prayer;
   To seek your salvation you've no time to spare.

You've time for earth's pleasures, for frolic and fun,
   For glittering treasures how quickly you run,
But care not to seek the fair mansions above,
   The favor of God or the gift of His love.

You've time to take voyages over the sea,
    And time to take in the gay world's jubilee;
But soon your bright hope will be lost in the gloom
    Of the cold river of death, and the tomb.

You've time to resort to woods, mountains, and glen,
    And time to gain knowledge from books and from men.
Yet no time to search for the wisdom of God:
    But what of your soul when you're under the sod?

For time will not linger when helpless you lie;
    Staring death in the face you will take time to die!
Then, what of the Judgment? Pause, think, I implore!
    For time will be lost on eternity's shore.

—Author Unknown

RECOMMENDATION

"Ye therefore, beloved, seeing ye know these things before, beware lest ye also, being led away with the error of the wicked, fall from your own stedfastness. But grow in grace, and in the knowledge of our Lord and Saviour Jesus Christ. To Him be glory both now and for ever. Amen."—2 Peter 3:17-18

Very suddenly the apostle concludes his Epistle. Though using only a few words in his closing remarks, he has much to say. Last words are usually important words. This is certainly true in 2 Peter. In the light of the prevailing apostasy which the apostle has so sharply condemned, he makes two important recommendations to the children of God in his final appeal: first, to stand true; secondly, to grow strong.

The Apostle Peter has given us a clear-cut warning of apostasy and its evils. At the same time he has emphasized the fact that one of the apostate's strongest attacks is launched against the doctrine of the visible, bodily return of Jesus Christ. With this in mind, he says to those who are in Christ: "Ye therefore, beloved, seeing ye know these things before, beware lest ye also, being led away with the error of the wicked, fall from your own stedfastness."

"Steadfastness" embodies the thought of following resolutely and unswervingly in one direction. Those who have been born from above, through the quickening power of the Holy Spirit, should evidence their new life and transformation by heading boldly in one direction. Second Peter makes it unmistakably clear as to what this direction is; it is the upward way that has the "blessed hope" as its satisfying and consoling assurance. Though the upward way has its trials and struggles, it is not without its encouragements, the greatest of which is the Second Coming of Christ.

Thus Peter exhorts us in his closing thoughts to stand true, lest through submitting to the devil's beguiling and subtle schemes we should stumble from the upward way to the lower. In warning us the apostle uses the word "beware." This means to *keep on your guard*. It is a military term used in reference to something of extreme value, being watched over and protected by armed soldiers. In Ephesians 6:11 God exhorts each of us to "put on the whole armour of God, that ye may be able to stand against the wiles of the devil." We must be clothed with the Christian's armor lest Satan should get an advantage over us. To be sure, he is using scores of diabolical means in his attempt to turn the Lord's people from the upward way, the way of righteousness and holiness. So often Satan is successful because believers do not remain steadfast. They fail to keep resolutely following in the Lord's direction.

It has been a most gratifying pleasure in my Bible conference ministry to have the privilege of conducting special services in various churches in many parts of our country. In these churches I have met outstanding men and women of God who are being used in a mighty way to serve the Lord. In returning to some of these churches a year or so later, for another series of meetings, I have noticed that some of these friends who seemed to be so zealous and busy for God were no longer in attendance. Inquiring as to their whereabouts, I have seen many a pastor frown and shake his head in disappointment, only to say, "They are no longer walking with the Lord." Think of it! These who were once ardent soul winners, devoted Bible lovers, dedicated saints, are now defeated and useless. How does one explain this? Has the Lord failed? Such would be impossible. Look at God's assuring words in Psalm 89:33, "Nevertheless My lovingkindness will I not utterly take from him, nor suffer My faithfulness to fail." God cannot possibly fail. But His people can; and we have failed many, many times. Why is it that we have found ourselves growing cold in heart, lacking in a sincere concern to do a work for God? Simply because we have overlooked the importance of focusing our vision in the proper direction, the upward way, "looking for that blessed hope, and the glorious appearing of the great God and our Saviour Jesus Christ" (Titus 2:13). Paul could say, "forgetting those things which are behind, and reaching forth unto those things which are before, I press toward the mark for the prize of the high calling of God in Christ Jesus" (Philippians 3:13-14). This is an example of the same steadfastness which Peter is recommending to you and to me. Until Christ comes, let us be steadfast, moving resolutely with purpose and determination in one direction—the way of the Lord.

While traveling, several years ago, I met a Christian young man I had not seen for a long time. Among other things, I inquired as to the welfare of his dad. In former years I had come to know his father very well and had learned to love him in the Lord because of his zeal and strong witness for the Lord. This friend had experienced a remarkable conversion late in life. Almost immediately he went to work for God, lifting high the banner of Christ, serving the Lord faithfully. His was a practical faith. He began to pour his business profits, as well as much of his own income, into the Lord's work. He faithfully gave witness to Christ in churches, missions, and wherever an opportunity opened. Many came to know the Lord because of his clear-cut and Christ-centered testimony for Christ. When I asked the young son about his father, he bowed his head and said slowly, "I am afraid we have an alcoholic on our hands. Dad has drifted back." Oh, how those words pierced my heart. What grief, to realize that here was another great victory for the devil—a child of God failed to remain steadfast.

Such is not uncommon or unusual. It is happening every day simply because so many of the Lord's people take too much for granted. Often, believers try to live on past experiences. I know this to be true, for so often I hear Christians boasting of what they once did or what they once were for God. If we are to be steadfast for the Lord we must have a fresh experience with Him daily. If we do not, we shall soon grow cold at heart and as the result we shall no longer be able to stand against the enemy's thrust. In 1 Corinthians 10:12 God records a most solemn and vital warning for every believer in Christ, "Wherefore let him that thinketh he standeth take heed lest he fall." God is speaking here not to some Christians but to all Christians. Any one of us could fall back into sin and into the old paths from which the Lord salvaged us. Only neglect to remain steadfast, and defeat will surely come. Failing to go forward with the Lord always results in retreat with the devil.

Considering this theme of steadfastness, there is another aspect of it that must not be overlooked. Frequently believers feel that they must keep themselves steadfast. Be assured, steadfastness, like any other grace taught in the Word of God, demands complete dependence upon Jesus Christ. We cannot save ourselves, nor can we keep ourselves steadfast. Most of us have tried to keep steadfast in our own strength at some time in the past, but we have failed miserably. The secret of victory is found in Hebrews 12:1-2: "Wherefore seeing we also are compassed about with so great a cloud of witnesses, let us lay aside every weight, and the sin which doth so easily beset us, and let us run with patience the race that is set before us, Looking unto Jesus the author and finisher of our faith; who for the joy that was set before Him endured the cross, despising the shame, and is set down at the right hand of the throne of God."

Who of us could begin to deal with "weights" and "sins" in our own strength and ability? The slightest attempt would produce only failure, for the task is too big for any of us. Feeling we have successfully dealt with one sin, we might turn to another. But soon the old sin breaks out again in another manner, usually in a worse and uglier form. How then can we be steadfast? Is it a hopeless problem? Looking to ourselves it is, but the writer of Hebrews says we must look unto Jesus. He alone is our source of strength and help. There is no temptation too potent for Him to overcome. Nor is there any sin He cannot banish. Look unto Him with your weaknesses! Look unto Him with your failures! Look unto Him with your heartaches! Let there not be a time when you do not look unto Him.

Looking unto Him, "Let us run with patience the race that is set before us." The secret of successful running is proper preparation. We must go to our Lord daily, boldly confessing our impotence and helplessness. With sincerity, our treacherous hearts must be laid bare before God, recognizing His all-sufficiency. We need a constant realization of the complete worthlessness of the flesh and its deceitful ways. Before the Lord will do His mighty and miraculous works through us, self needs to be crucified and the Spirit given unqualified leadership and control. The job can be done in no other way. The glory is all of the Lord. Oh, let us die to ourselves, remembering the secret, "Looking unto Jesus!" This is God's plan. When temptation comes, when the devil attacks and the pull seems almost unbearable, lift your heart in the thick of the battle and say, "Lord, it is up to You. I cannot do it, but You can." Help will come immediately. He has promised that "There hath no temptation taken you but such as is common to man: but God is faithful, who will not suffer you to be tempted above that ye are able; but will with the temptation also make a way to escape, that ye may be able to bear it" (1 Corinthians 10:13). Do not miss those words, "God is faithful." There is no hope in us; but there is in Him. He will "make a way to escape." Trust Him! Believe Him! Look to Him! Obey Him! "Be ye stedfast, unmovable, always abounding in the work of the Lord, forasmuch as ye know that your labour is not in vain in the Lord" (1 Corinthians 15:58). Nothing is "in vain in the Lord." But it must be "in the Lord," not in us.

Not only is the saint of God required to be steadfast, but he is to grow strong in the Lord. Peter says, "But grow in grace, and in the knowledge of our Lord and Saviour Jesus Christ." How necessary this recommendation is! Is it not true that numbers of our present-day churches have followed the false teachers into apostasy because there are so many in those churches who, though born again, have remained as spiritual babes. Failing to feed on the strong meat of God's truth and neglecting the sincere milk of the Word, they have not matured in the faith. These spiritual infants are found not only in liberal churches, but in all churches. They are a constant source of grief to their pastors' hearts. They need so much attention and care. Like little babies, they get hurt easily. They cry and whine when things do not go their way. They demand special handling and help. Feeble and weak, they cannot walk long or far without falling. Oh how tragic it is to see Christians remaining as babies for ten, twenty, thirty years, and even more. They have not grown in the Lord. To them Peter declares, "But grow in grace, and in the knowledge of our Lord and Saviour Jesus Christ."

The reason for this sad state is that they have not been men and women of the Book, the Word of God. They have been too busy, or too uninterested to take time to wait on the Lord. If one is to grow he must have food. This is true of our children in our homes, if they are to have sound, robust bodies. The same is true spiritually. Many of God's people want to be strong Christians. They desire to be leaders; they long to be witnesses for Christ. But they are trying to grow without eating. This is an impossibility. If one is a weak, defeated, unhappy Christian, doubtless it is because he is not spending adequate time waiting on God, studying His Word, seeking His purposes and plans for his life.

I had just spoken in the Sunday evening service of a church in the Midwest when a young man approached me and asked if he could have a few minutes of my time for counseling. Gladly I consented and invited him to come with me to the pastor's study. After we had seated ourselves, I asked, "What seems to be your problem?"

"I am a pastor," he said, "but I must confess that I am miserable and dissatisfied." He told me about his church and then said, "It seems as though my ministry has been a failure. Preaching and the work of the church seem to be such a burden and a chore. I lack the joy I once had in the service of the Lord. Worst of all," he said, "I see no fruit." He continued on at length acquainting me with some of the problems of his church and his own personal life. I listened attentively, but at the same time I prayed for wisdom that the Lord would enable me to help him. By the time he finished, a question came to my mind, which I asked immediately.

"How much time do you spend waiting on God with your Bible and prayer each morning before you enter into the responsibilities and duties of your pastorate?" It seemed like minutes, but it was probably only seconds, that he simply sat staring at me. Finally, as though God had found him out, he spoke up saying, "Well, I guess that's it. That's my sin. I don't like to get up in the morning." After further discussion, we found that this was the sin Satan was using to keep this young pastor from a life of usefulness for God. Rather than disciplining his life by setting the hour to meet God, he merely arose when he awakened, which was usually too late to spend adequate time with the Lord. Off he would rush into his work without drawing on the much-needed resources of God. Small wonder that he was in such a frame of mind.

It is quite obvious that many of God's servants are failing because of this same sin—the neglect of spending time with God. Be sure, we can do little for Him unless we take time to be with Him. Have you lost the joy you once had in the fellowship of your Lord? Is it a burden to serve Him? Do you find it much easier to do what you want rather than what God wants? Possibly you have grown cold in heart. You may even be bitter about something. No one knows it but you and God. You are still going through the motions of serving the Lord, but inwardly there is rebellion and misery. There is a solution! Submit at this very moment to Christ's complete control of your life. Look unto Jesus! Only as you do this can you become a blessing for God.

Consider this parable from the common, ordinary floor mop. The sponge floor mops are quite an improvement over the old, drippy rag mops with which we used to struggle. But sponge mops are dry, hard, and useless until immersed in water. It is fascinating to see the change as they soften, expand, and become usable. The sponge doesn't work at taking in the water; it needs only to be immersed in it. It just absorbs it until it becomes completely saturated. If we were to take a sincere inward look at ourselves as Christians, some of us would quickly realize that our lives are barren and useless. We would see them as they are, dry and crusty, difficult to live with, fruitless and empty. Possibly we are worn out "trying" to live the Christian life and frustrated that our service for God is so ineffective. Take a lesson from the lowly sponge mop. Turn to the source of Living Water, the Lord Jesus Christ, and drink until you are completely saturated with Him. Then and only then will Christian service be a joy and an inspiration.

Would you continue to grow in grace and in the understanding of our Lord and Saviour Jesus Christ? Then establish the quiet time with God as a principle you will not break, a must for your daily schedule. As soon as possible in the morning, preferably the first thing, meet God, that your needy soul may receive the Bread of Life and the Water of Life to sustain you in the service of our wonderful Saviour. In Colossians 1:27 Paul makes the statement, "Christ in you, the hope of glory." Here is an indispensable truth. What we are, what we do, what we have is dependent upon the measure to which we commit our lives to Christ and draw upon His mighty power. He will give as much as we are willing to receive. He will control only what we surrender to Him. How much of you does He have at this very moment? Are you a babe in Christ or are you growing and abounding in His marvelous grace?

As Peter concludes, he points all of us to the only true fountainhead of blessing and happiness: "To Him be glory both now and for ever. Amen." What a wonderful conclusion to the Epistle. In fact, this is a wonderful way to conclude everything. When we lay our heads on our pillows at night, quickly scanning over the many events of the day, we should be able to say, "To Him be glory both now and forever." If anything was done without honor and glory to Him, it was time hopelessly wasted. Whatever it might be—gains or losses, successes or failures, joys or sorrows, health or sickness, the true believer can say with Peter, "To Him be glory, both now and forever." How blessed it is to come to the end of one's life and be able to look back over the years spent walking with Him and serving Him, then to be able to say, "To Him be glory both now and forever." Such an experience demands a full commitment to Him.

As Peter closes his Epistle, so I conclude this series by pointing to the One who enabled me to prepare these messages. My earnest prayer and desire is that "To Him be glory, both now and forever." If God has spoken to you at all, praise Him. Give all glory and honor to whom it belongs. This you can do only as you know Him. Do you belong to Him? You say you are a Christian, but is your life and everything you have really His?

A missionary from Africa says that the greatest prayer he ever heard an African pray was from the lips of a Negro woman who had just recently become a Christian: "O

Thou great Chief, light a fire in my heart so I can see to sweep the rubbish out of Thy dwelling place." There is no question about it, this earnest soul meant business with the Lord. May the same be true of us. Believer in Christ, let us pay the price. At this very moment bow your head and let the Lord do in you what He desires to do. We need His fullness more than anything else. He fills only empty vessels. David must have realized this as he prayed in Psalm 51:7, "Purge me with hyssop, and I shall be clean: wash me, and I shall be whiter than snow." May this be our desire—to be "clean . . . whiter than snow." Let us ask God to purge from us all that is hindering His fullness and to wash us clean from everything that is staining our testimony for Him. Let us give ourselves to Him afresh, that He might take us and use us as His chosen ones, His possessions.

It is possible that you have read all these messages but still you do not know Him as your Saviour and Lord. I have sought to uphold Christ. But knowledge about Christ is meaningless unless you receive Him into your heart. Christ is the only way of salvation. Peter says, "To *Him* be glory." It is not to our good works "be glory," nor to our good life "be glory." It is Christ who must receive all glory. When God's blood-bought children reach Heaven they will sing, not about what they have done, not about what they have been; they will sing about Him, the Lord Jesus. In Revelation 5:9-10 we read: "And they sung a new song, saying, Thou art worthy to take the book, and to open the seals thereof: for Thou wast slain, and hast redeemed us to God by thy blood out of every kindred, and tongue, and people, and nation; And hast made us unto our God kings and priests: and we shall reign on the earth." It is Christ who will be the central theme of eternity's song. You will never praise Him in eternity unless you praise Him now. Oh, come, sinner friend, come to Christ! Believe on Him now! Let Him unfold to you a brilliant future, filled to overflowing with His greatness. Forget the past; start living anew with the Lord Jesus. Give yourself to Him.